How to Lead It:
Primary Geography

Other titles from Bloomsbury Education

How to Lead It: Primary English by Tricia Moss and Sallie Stanton
How to Lead It: Primary Maths by Shannen Doherty
How to Lead It: Primary Science by Kirsty Simkin
How to Lead It: Primary History by Alex Pethick
The Curriculum Compendium by Rae Snape
What Every Teacher Needs to Know by Jade Pearce

How to Lead It: Primary Geography

Emma Lennard
Series editor: Jon Hutchinson

BLOOMSBURY EDUCATION
LONDON OXFORD NEW YORK NEW DELHI SYDNEY

BLOOMSBURY EDUCATION
Bloomsbury Publishing Plc
50 Bedford Square, London WC1B 3DP, UK
Bloomsbury Publishing Ireland Limited
29 Earlsfort Terrace, Dublin 2, D02 AY28, Ireland

BLOOMSBURY, BLOOMSBURY EDUCATION and the Diana logo are trademarks of
Bloomsbury Publishing Plc

First published in Great Britain, 2025 by Bloomsbury Publishing Plc
This edition published in Great Britain, 2025 by Bloomsbury Publishing Plc

A catalogue record for this book is available from the British Library

ISBN: PB: 978-1-80199-624-2; ePDF: 978-1-80199-625-9; ePub: 978-1-80199-622-8

2 4 6 8 10 9 7 5 3 1 (paperback)

Cover design by Sophie Gordon

Typeset by Newgen KnowledgeWorks Pvt. Ltd., Chennai, India
Printed and bound in the UK by CPI Group (UK) Ltd., Croydon, CR0 4YY

MIX
Paper | Supporting
responsible forestry
FSC® C013604

To find out more about our authors and books visit www.bloomsbury.com
and sign up for our newsletters

For product safety related questions contact productsafety@bloomsbury.com

Contents

Acknowledgements

My heartfelt thanks to Joanna Ramsay and Jon Hutchinson for their support throughout the process of writing, and for their careful editing of this book. Thank you also to the many teachers and leaders in schools who I work with every day; you are truly inspirational. Finally, thank you to my family for your patience and encouragement, I am so fortunate to be on this journey with you.

1 Leading geography

Where am I? What is around me? Where can I go? What might I find there? Many of the children in our schools will ask important questions such as these as they journey through their early childhood, seeking to understand where they are in the world and wondering what lies beyond their experiences. Whilst leading geography in our school, we have a unique opportunity to help pupils answer these questions.

Geography can mean many things to a young child, from knowing what is located in and around their school to understanding that there are places far, far away. It can mean understanding the shape of land, that it can be flat or very steep, and that rivers run through it as they journey to the sea. Geography can be about people: where they live, why they live there and how they have changed the land around them. When pupils study geography in primary school, they are invited to explore the world, understand how people interact with the natural world, and look for ways in which places and people around the world are connected.

As teachers, when we lead this fascinating and multifaceted subject, we can ask ourselves what a pupil's geography experience looks like as they journey from their early years through their primary education. We can reflect on the foundation that their primary geography education creates for future learning. Importantly, we should consider geography's role in developing a child's identity. Geography is not just about maps and locations; it's about connecting children to their world, fostering a sense of belonging and agency to impact the world around them.

This chapter will explore:

- what is geography?
- the role of a primary geography subject leader
- understanding knowledge in primary geography
- how this book can support you.

What is geography?

Professor Peter Jackson explains that geography can be thought of as a language, one that provides a way of thinking about the world. Languages have both vocabulary and grammar which together help to construct meaning. If the vocabulary of geography is the geographical information we teach, the grammar is the 'big ideas' which help us to connect that information and understand it. At the annual conference of the Geographical Association in 2006, Professor Peter Jackson suggested that the following 'big ideas' are relevant for children of any age who encounter geography:

- 'space and place' – ways in which humans use space to create places with meaning
- 'scale and connection' – how both people and places are connected from a local to a global scale
- 'proximity and difference' – how the world is becoming more connected, with distances appearing to shrink with the advent of technology that connects us so closely regardless of physical distance
- 'relational thinking' – how our view of the world is determined by our perspective.

As primary leaders, it is helpful for us to have a clear understanding of geography and how it contributes to young children's understanding of the world around them.

The role of a primary geography subject leader

You may have found yourself leading geography even though you don't necessarily have qualifications or experience in the subject. But with the right planning and preparation, you can lead geography effectively. Here, I outline the key aspects of the role and suggest leadership questions for you to focus on.

1. Curriculum Development

Developing your school's geography curriculum will involve:

- being clear on the intent of geography in your school
- overseeing curriculum content and structure; ensuring the curriculum is specified and sequenced to support progression

- ensuring a consistent approach to enactment (teaching) of the geography curriculum
- implementing effective assessment systems to monitor pupil progress and curriculum impact
- ensuring an inclusive geography curriculum that supports all pupils, no matter their starting point or additional needs
- keeping up to date on relevant research related to the teaching of primary geography.

Leadership questions

- What do pupils learn in our geography curriculum?
- How is geography taught across our school?
- How do we check on pupil progress?
- How do we support all pupils to access the curriculum?
- Where do I look for updates within the geography education community?

2. Raising standards and achieving consistency

Monitoring teaching and learning to assess how well geography is being implemented across the school, and how consistently well it is delivered, can be achieved through:

- utilising data analysis (although be cautious about the accuracy of the data generated by your school – we explore this further in Chapter 9: Assessment)
- taking learning walks
- observing lessons
- checking planning
- engaging with pupil voice, using informal interviews with small groups of children, conversations with the school council or pupils' questionnaires
- reviewing a small sample of pupils' books from each class (depending on your priorities you could select samples from target groups, such as Pupil Premium)
- devising staff and pupil questionnaires.

Leadership questions

- How do I check on primary geography in my school?
- Do we collect data on pupil progress or attainment in geography? How is that data generated? What does it tell us? What is the impact on teacher workload?
- What do pupils and teachers say about geography? What do pupils enjoy? What do teachers like teaching?
- What is the impact of the geography curriculum?
- Which areas of teaching and learning in geography could be developed?

3. Supporting colleagues

You can foster a supportive working environment by:

- being the go-to person for any geography-based queries, and knowing where to seek answers
- guiding staff through teaching, learning, resources, planning and assessment
- offering feedback and professional development, based on information gathered through subject monitoring
- modelling the teaching of geography, where possible.

Leadership questions

- How well do you know the content of the geography curriculum across the school?
- If a teacher needs support with subject knowledge (for example how to teach scale or coordinates), how can you support them? Do you know where to signpost?
- How do you decide what the focus is for geography professional development?

4. Resourcing

Planning and acquiring resources for your subject will involve:

- managing the geography subject budget effectively, allocating funding where it is needed to support teaching and learning

- pursuing additional funding from external sources, when needed
- auditing and updating resources needed to deliver the curriculum and ensuring these align with pupil needs
- providing access to safety guidance and risk assessment information for fieldwork
- supporting teachers to gain confidence with subject knowledge.

Leadership questions

- What are the costs associated with implementing your geography curriculum?
- What resources do teachers need to deliver the curriculum? (For example Ordnance Survey (OS) maps, atlases, compasses.)
- What would be helpful to have available in the staffroom for teachers? (For example books, journals, geography magazines.)

Understanding knowledge in primary geography

The primary geography curriculum teaches geographical knowledge that pupils will apply in different contexts in the classroom and during fieldwork. This knowledge will equip pupils to think geographically, from locating places to understanding what is in that place, using map skills, looking for patterns and making connections. David Lambert explains that geography has both vocabulary (the facts and knowledge of the world), and grammar (concepts that help us to make sense of those facts) (Lambert, 2011, pp.243-264). An example of this would be knowing that oranges don't grow in England because it isn't warm enough, but that global trade brings them from other warmer countries to our supermarkets. This use of both geography's vocabulary and grammar together supports pupils to think geographically.

Peter Jackson describes thinking geographically as 'a uniquely powerful way of seeing the world' (Jackson, 2006, p.13). He explains that thinking in this way 'can help us see the connections between places and scales that others frequently miss.'

Knowledge within the primary curriculum has several important forms that it is helpful to be aware of:

- **Substantive knowledge:** This is the content within the curriculum, for example there are seven continents, the United Kingdom is in the northern hemisphere, and the coastline is where land meets the sea. Understanding what substantive knowledge is within our primary geography curriculum helps us to gain clarity over curriculum content. This helps us ensure that content is sequenced effectively to support pupils in learning and remembering more over time.

- **Disciplinary knowledge:** This relates to 'knowledge of how geographical knowledge is formed, debated and contested' (Ofsted 2023). For primary pupils, this relates to how we know things about the world, what questions geographers ask and how they answer them. It might involve asking pupils: 'what might a geographer say about this place? What might a geographer notice?'

- **Procedural knowledge:** This is the knowledge needed to undertake geography. This could be reading symbols on a map, drawing sketch maps, using coordinates, calculating distance using a scale, using a map to navigate, gathering data, and analysing data. Procedural knowledge can often be taught explicitly in the classroom, enabling pupils to master the procedures needed to be successful, and then applied in practice during fieldwork.

As a leader of primary geography, it is helpful to understand how these three forms of knowledge are woven through the curriculum. Consider what pupils learn in geography, what they understand about how geographical knowledge has been established, and what they need to know in order to understand and practise geography effectively.

When leading geography, an important consideration is the immediate experience the pupils in your school have of the world. What do we know about the lives our children lead? They may live on farmland, spending much of their time outside, or in the inner city, experiencing an urban childhood. They may have opportunities to travel widely, or their world might be limited to a small geographical area. Reflecting on your pupils' experiences will help you to shape your geography curriculum so that it can support your pupils to connect to the wider world in a meaningful way.

How this book can support you

This book has been structured for you, a busy subject leader, to dip into throughout your time leading geography. It aims to explain some key elements of your role and provide ideas for developing and delivering a quality primary geography curriculum.

Within this book, you will find digestible summaries of research and ideas for the practical application of this within primary geography. There are case studies to help put some of the research and knowledge into context, alongside suggestions for professional development. Key questions will support you to focus your thinking about geography in your schools and will encourage critical analysis of the strengths and areas for improvement.

In this book you will find:

- examples of best practice across key stages
- real and fictional case studies
- suggestions for staff professional development
- reflection questions to help you structure your thoughts and identify next steps
- follow-up reading and resources if you want to explore a particular area further.

I hope this book acts as a companion for you as you lead geography in your school.

Chapter summary

- Our primary geography curriculum can offer children a space to consider important questions such as: *Where am I? What is around me? Where can I go? What might I find there?*
- As leaders, is it helpful for us to consider the context from which children are beginning their geographical education and think about a young child's early experiences of the world around them.
- Your role as a geography leader may involve:
  - Curriculum development
  - Raising standards and achieving consistency
  - Supporting colleagues
  - Resourcing

- Understanding knowledge in the primary curriculum involves consideration of substantive, disciplinary and procedural knowledge. All three of these elements of knowledge work together to support understanding in geography.

Questions for reflection

The following questions for reflection are a good place to start as you embark upon leading geography in your school. They will help you to gain a clear picture of children's experiences of the world so far and will help you to understand how the geography curriculum can build on these.

- Where do our pupils live?
- What do our pupils experience in the world around them?
- What do we have available in our local area for our pupils to experience?

Explore further

- Peter Jackson's article 'Thinking geographically' in *The Geographical Association Conference Paper* (2006)
- *Debates in Geography Education* (2017), edited by David Lambert and Mark Jones
- *Teaching Primary Geography* (2017) by Stephen Scoffham and Paula Owens

2 Getting the best from research evidence

As geography subject leaders, our core responsibility is to ensure we have high-quality teaching and good pupil outcomes in our subject. It is important that you base your decisions and practice upon evidence, using robust and reliable educational research to decide which are the most effective strategies for your setting.

The challenge is how to sift through the research, identify what works, why it works and how to use it to improve classroom practice in geography. The principles and resources laid out in this chapter aim to support you in your quest to ensure that the primary geography curriculum and its practice in classrooms are based on robust and reliable evidence.

This chapter will explore:

- educational research – where do we start?
- guiding principles – how to engage with research
- primary education sources and guidance – where to look for useful research
- geography-specific sources and guidance.

This chapter may be read with Chapter 3 which looks more closely at research evidence around cognitive science and its implications for primary geography.

Educational research

Educational research is a broad field where evidence and data are systematically collected and analysed. Research can involve various methods and can look into many different aspects of education. For example, a study could look at a specific pedagogical tool, such as questioning, or it could look at a broader topic, such as effective early reading instruction. One of the challenges of engaging with educational research is that it can be conducted using different standards, criteria and ways of working. Educational research may focus on a topic related to economics, psychology, philosophy or other disciplines; its scope, as you can see is very broad.

Many research studies in education are limited by the characteristics and context of the participants; classrooms are not laboratories, and it is hard to control all factors. For example, if we were comparing the impact of a maths intervention in two different classrooms, the cohort of children would not be identical. There could be more summer-born children in one cohort which might impact the results, some children might be absent for part of the study, children could leave the school and new children join. There are many challenges for educational researchers to overcome when producing reliable and robust research.

When engaging with research we must consider how applicable that research is to the context within which we are working. These are some useful questions to think about:

- Who participated in the research?
- What age children did the research focus on?
- What education system was the research conducted within? For example, was the research undertaken abroad? If so, we must bear in mind international differences.

Although educational research is complex and not without challenges, there is a wealth of research available that has interesting implications for us as leaders within primary schools and we will look at some of it together in this book. Dr Ben Goldacre, a doctor and academic, said, 'By collecting better evidence about what works best, and establishing a culture where this evidence is used as a matter of routine, we can improve outcomes for children and increase professional independence' (2013, p.4). So, how can we find out what works best while juggling the demands of our classroom-based roles? Fortunately, there are some tools to support us with this important work and we will explore some of these in this chapter.

Guiding principles

When you are considering how best to approach educational research, you need to think about what the research is telling you and how it applies to your own school context. What does this evidence mean for the teachers and pupils in your school?

The time you have available to think about research, engage with professional development and support others in implementing evidence-based practice will be limited. So, it is important to use your time effectively. The following approaches can be helpful in guiding decisions:

- **Prioritise large-scale studies**: Focus on research with substantial sample sizes. How an intervention worked for the pupils within a study is irrelevant if the same intervention is unlikely to work for your own pupils. Bigger samples tend to allow for more generalisable conclusions, leading to interventions appropriate for a wider range of learners.

- **Consider the consistency of the participants**: A large sample size doesn't automatically guarantee high-quality research. You should also examine the participant selection process and drop-out rates: long-term studies based on primary pupils are prone to changes in participants as pupils and/or teachers move schools. Much research is also conducted on secondary-school pupils and undergraduates, so be cautious of applying findings about older pupils to those in primary or EYFS.

- **Compare contexts**: It is always important to look at context when putting good ideas into practice. Even when research shows something works well, what worked before doesn't guarantee future success (Major & Higgins 2019). You should also think carefully about whether particular ideas are right for your situation. Your school might have special challenges that could make a new idea harder to use, for example, and you might need to do some preparation work to help it succeed. Before introducing a new idea, consider if it's possible for you, if you can afford it, and if you can keep it going. Often, it's easier to change what you're already doing instead of starting something completely new. This can save money and make it easier for people to accept and use a new idea.

- **Be wary of simplification**: Research that has been distilled into bite-sized chunks can lead us to decisions we believe are perfect fits for our schools. However, we should remember that broadly generalised results, especially those summarised without nuance, can only really give us an 'average effect' impression.

- **Don't trust results implicitly**: We should be mindful that all findings are built on a body of research that can be later questioned as more research studies are published. The dynamic nature of research means that leaders may need to keep updating their understanding. The best way to keep on top of relevant updates is to sign up the newsletters of trusted organisations (some of which are recommended below). This way you will get a regular reminder to engage with the newest findings.

- **Steer clear of educational fallacies**: The field of education is rife with myths, misconceptions and outdated ideas – for example, that pupils will learn better if they discover things for themselves, or that repetition is the surest way to secure understanding. Many of these persist despite being disproven (de Bruyckere et al., 2015). While you can't be aware of all of the fallacies, familiarising yourself with some common ones can save time, helping you to focus on more-promising approaches. (See the 'Explore further' section at the end of this chapter for some recommended reading on this.)

If you are a subject leader who is new to appraising evidence, you might want to start by looking at the Institute for Effective Education's *Engaging with evidence guide*, which breaks down different types of evidence and their limitations (Haslam & Shaw, 2019) or the EEF's *Using Research Evidence: A Concise Guide* (2024). The website 'That's a Claim!' (www.thatsaclaim.org/educational) is also helpful for bitesize explainers on different aspects of educational research.

Primary education sources and guidance

Engaging with educational research has the potential to transform classroom practice. Becoming research informed helps us to make better decisions in our classrooms and in our leadership roles, which leads to better outcomes for the pupils we teach and for the teachers we support. Reading research and analysing its findings, understanding statistical information, and interpreting specialist language may be challenging if we don't have prior experience working in this way. A good place to start is by engaging with the work of organisations that digest research and summarise complex evidence-based findings for teachers.

Some examples of where to start looking for evidence are outlined below:

The Education Endowment Foundation (EEF)

The EEF is an independent charity that was set up to improve educational attainment levels of pupils from lower socio-economic backgrounds in England. The Foundation helps schools, colleges and early-years settings improve outcomes through the better use of evidence. This may be through their guidance reports, which review the evidence base for a range of strategies developed to support specific areas. Alternatively, it may be through research into the efficacy of specific strategies.

- The *Teaching and Learning Toolkit* (EEF, 2021) is helpful when thinking about curriculum and lesson design, as well as how to support teachers to become more effective in their practice.
- *A School's Guide to Implementation* (Sharples et al., 2024) provides clear structures and systems that can help us when implementing new strategies in our schools.

The Nuffield Foundation

The Nuffield Foundation work to improve primary education outcomes and fund research into factors that impact upon educational opportunity. They undertake a broad range of research in pedagogy, assessment, school improvement and many more areas with an aim of understanding the different ways in which disadvantage can create barriers to education.

The Chartered College of Teaching

The Chartered College of Teaching is a professional body for teachers. Membership gives access to research, resources and the journal *Impact*. The College produces evidence summaries that review and collate research into short digests, and the journal has regular contributions from practitioners as well as researchers.

The Institute for Education Sciences (IES)

The IES is the independent, non-partisan statistics, research and evaluation arm of the US Department of Education. They conduct reviews on individual studies and grant access to a range of useful practice guides and intervention reports.

Geography-specific resources and guidance

As Professor Simon Catling acknowledges, 'There is research into younger children's geographical learning, but it is relatively limited' (Catling, 2013, p. 177). He goes on to explain that 'too many intentions and expectations for primary geography are based on hope, not evidence.' This poses a challenge for leaders of geography as there may not be a robust evidence base for some of the decisions we are making within our schools. However, educational research is a changing field, so as leaders we need to be willing and able to update our understanding as and when new research is released. Signing up for newsletters from the organisations below is a helpful way to ensure you are regularly reminded to engage with new findings. Following their accounts on social media or listening to related podcasts is also helpful.

When we explore research, we are engaging in reflective practice and opening our minds to adapting ways we work to become more effective. Professor Dylan Wiliam, said 'every teacher needs to improve, not because they are not good enough, but because they can be even better' (Wiliam, 2012). Getting the best from research evidence does not mean everything you do must be justified by research, sometimes you won't have a robust pool of evidence to draw from, but use research where it is available and where its conclusions are relevant to the context in which you work.

The Geographical Association

The Geographical Association work to support high-quality geography education. They publish regular journals that shine a light on research within geography education and its application in classrooms. They also host a range of professional development opportunities and other projects.

Their journal *Geography* (published since 1901) aims to bridge the gap between schools and research. It profiles current research in an accessible way. There is a subscription required for full access to this, but it might be possible for your school to allocate a small budget to cover this.

The Royal Geographical Society (RGS)

The RGS was founded in 1830 and its core purpose is to advance geographical science. As part of their work, the RGS supports geographical research and education. They work with teachers and schools as well as professional geographers.

Case study: engaging with sources and guidance

Farah works in a primary school in Yorkshire. The school are using the EEF's guidance report 'Improving Literacy in Key Stage 2' (Higgins et al., 2021) to think about how they support their pupils' progress in reading.

As geography lead, Farah wants to look for opportunities to build reading into the geography curriculum.

Using the EEF report, she identifies 'guided oral reading instruction' and 'repeated reading' as two evidence-based strategies for developing reading fluency. She undertakes some lesson observations. She notices that teachers do read text to pupils in geography, but that pupils are listening and not necessarily reading themselves.

Farah decides to trial some guided oral instruction in geography. She recognises that reading is not the main focus of a geography lesson, but sees an opportunity to reinforce good practice from English. She collates some short pieces of text relating to her geography topic, 'South America'. The texts include subject-specific vocabulary that she wants pupils to read with fluency. Farah models fluent reading of the text and her class then read the same text aloud together, echoing the way Farah read, her intonation, volume, speed and expression.

Farah plans to maintain this approach for a term before inviting the English leader to come and observe. They will then discuss what Farah has noticed about the impact of this strategy and if successful, Farah will lead a section of a staff meeting to disseminate the message. She will then support colleagues to implement this strategy in their own geography lessons.

Chapter summary

- Base decisions on reliable educational research, where it is available, considering both external evidence and internal data from your own context.

- When evaluating research, focus on large-scale studies with consistency of participants, be sure to consider studies' contexts, be wary of simplification and the fallibility of researchers, and be aware of common educational myths and misconceptions.

- Utilise resources and guides from reputable organisations like the EEF and subject-specific organisations such as the Geographical Association.

Questions for reflection

- In what ways do I currently engage with educational research in general?
- Do I engage with subject-specific research in geography?
- What professional development have I participated in for leading geography?
- Has this included research-based evidence?
- How could research evidence enhance my teaching of geography and subject leadership?

Example PD session: using research evidence

Here is an example of what a PD session on using research evidence could look like.

TIMING SUGGESTION	SESSION GUIDANCE
10 mins	Choose a piece of geography research to read together and understand, for example: 'Understanding of spatial correspondence does not contribute to representational understanding: evidence from the model Room and false belief tasks' by Catherine M. Sayer and Martin J. Doherty (2023). Summary: https://www.uea.ac.uk/about/news/article/can-children-map-read-at-the-age-of-four Full article: https://ueaeprints.uea.ac.uk/id/eprint/90133/1/DEV_2022_0355_R1_2_.pdf
5 mins	Discuss the research evidence with colleagues. What did the research find? What conclusions were drawn?

TIMING SUGGESTION	SESSION GUIDANCE
15 mins	Consider how this research may inform practice in geography. For example, how do pupils learn to use maps in Early Years Foundation Stage (EYFS) and Key Stage 1 (KS1)? Which maps are they being asked to use?
20 mins	Teachers consider how pupils make progress in understanding of maps within their year group and then work with colleagues to track that progress across key stages or phases.

Explore further

- *Using Research Evidence: A Concise Guide* (2024) by the Education Endowment Foundation
- 'Dispelling educational myths' (2017) by John Hattie
- Research in *Geography* 'Maps and cognitive maps: the young child's perception' (1979) by Simon Catling
- 'Maps and mapping in the early years: teaching map skills to inspire a sense of place and adventure in the early years' (2023) by Paula Owens

3 Cognitive science and implications for the classroom

In recent years, there has been a movement to combine findings from research into cognitive science (the science of how we learn) with classroom practice. This movement has caused many teachers to reflect upon their pedagogy (how they teach) whilst considering what cognitive science tells us about how we can support pupils' learning.

There are many books, blogs, and articles about cognitive science that will help leaders reflect on their practice, and at the end of this chapter, you can find some recommended reading. In this chapter, we will consider some key pieces of research and how they have the potential to impact the teaching of geography in our schools.

The EEF commissioned a systematic evidence and practice review in 2021, which looked at the evidence base surrounding cognitive science and its application in the classroom. It produced a report for teachers which outlines seven different aspects of cognitive science and how they may be applied in the classroom (Perry et al., 2021).

In this chapter, we will look at the seven areas identified by the EEF review and consider their implications for the primary geography curriculum. These seven areas are:

1. spaced learning
2. interleaving
3. retrieval practice
4. managing cognitive load
5. working with schemas
6. multimedia learning (including dual coding)
7. embodied learning

1. Spaced learning

Spaced learning or spaced practice is a way of organising learning and practice where study is spread out over time, allowing pupils to revisit previously learned content that they may have forgotten. This contrasts with massed practice where content is studied in one block.

This approach was developed from the work of Herman Ebbinghaus, a German researcher working in the 1800s who was interested in memory. He is known for his study into memory that involved him learning lists of 'nonsense syllables' – strings of letters with one syllable that are not real words. He noticed that by spacing out his practice sessions, he could reduce the number of syllables he was forgetting over time, therefore learning more effectively (Ebbinghaus, 1885).

This research shows that pupils forget content, but by asking pupils to remember the content we have taught them spaced out between intervals, we can increase the amount they remember over time. One of the reasons why spacing may be effective for pupils' learning is because it increases what is known as 'storage strength', a way in which information is effectively stored in our long-term memory (Bjork et al., 1992).

Implications for the geography curriculum

Spaced learning potentially has implications for at least two aspects of primary geography: how the curriculum is designed and sequenced, and how individual geography lessons are structured.

Curriculum design and sequence

When considering your curriculum design and sequence, it could be helpful to look at when pupils revisit content. For example, pupils could learn about 'rivers' in one individual unit and then move on to other content, with little or no opportunity to revisit their knowledge of rivers. Alternatively, recognising the impact of spaced learning, pupils could study 'rivers' as an individual unit, then revisit it in multiple contexts when studying the UK, Europe and the wider world.

Structuring individual lessons

Spaced learning could support pupils' learning of new vocabulary within a lesson and across several lessons. By building in time into your lesson structures for revisiting prior learning and planning opportunities for retrieval (asking pupils to remember previously taught content), such as through quizzing, you can support pupils' memory, leading to effective learning over time.

Reflect on your curriculum offer

The table below illustrates how to use knowledge of spaced learning to reflect on your geography curriculum offer.

Curriculum content	Reflection questions	Example	Considerations
Introducing new vocabulary within a lesson	How is new vocabulary taught in geography lessons?	*'We teach the list of new vocabulary at the beginning of the lesson.'* *'We teach new vocabulary at the beginning of the lesson and then revisit the key words throughout the lesson.'* *'We look at the vocabulary for a whole unit, assign relevant vocabulary to each lesson, which is taught and then revisited throughout the lesson, and we also quiz pupils on words from previous lessons and from previous units.'*	Is pupils' learning of vocabulary in geography spaced effectively? Do they revisit previously learned words later when at risk of forgetting? Do we space practice of key vocabulary across lessons, units, year groups and beyond?
Local geography across the curriculum	When do pupils learn about local geography in our curriculum?	*'We have a local geography unit in Year 4.'* *'We have one local geography unit in KS1 and one in KS2.'* *'All pupils study a unit that includes some local geography in each year group in KS1 and KS2.'*	When pupils learn about local geography, where is their prior knowledge coming from? When do pupils revisit and build on their knowledge of local geography?

Curriculum content	Reflection questions	Example	Considerations
British geography across the curriculum	Where does British geography feature in our curriculum?	'Pupils learn about Britain in Year 1.' 'We have one British geography unit in lower Key Stage 2 that studies human geography and another in upper Key Stage 2 that studies physical geography.' 'Pupils in EYFS learn about the UK and begin to look at maps. They build on that in Key Stage 1, learning more physical and human features, and again in Key Stage 2 when they look in more detail about geographical issues such as flooding.'	When are pupils introduced to the UK? What do pupils learn about the UK and when? How does pupils' knowledge of the UK build over time?
World geography across the curriculum	When do pupils learn about world geography within our curriculum?	'In KS1, pupils study San Francisco and in KS2 they study North America.' 'In KS1, pupils study the seven continents. They revisit this knowledge each year when focussing on particular regions of the world.'	Could pupils learn about a place and not revisit it again, therefore making forgetting very likely? How does the curriculum build on pupils' knowledge of the world over time?

2. Interleaving

Interleaving is the practice of switching between different but related types of problems or ideas within the same lesson or period of learning, such as a half term.

Implications for the geography curriculum

Research into this has largely focused on mathematics education, where pupils might switch between operations, for example, working on multiplication and division within one lesson, requiring different but related knowledge. Using interleaving when teaching new content, may not be a useful strategy for primary geography as it may risk confusing pupils if related content is presented without recognising the differences. However interleaving questions relating to previously taught topics might be helpful when planning retrieval quizzes.

3. Retrieval practice

Retrieval practice involves remembering something you have learned in the past, and thinking about it (Weinstein et al., 2019). It is about bringing something to mind. This is what happens when we ask pupils to revisit something they have learned before. Retrieval practice works hand in hand with spaced practice and therefore can both be a tool for learning and to assess learning.

Implications for the geography curriculum

Examples of retrieval practice in primary geography:

- a blank map of the world is displayed and pupils are asked to name the seven continents and five oceans
- a multiple-choice quiz with questions linked to content from the last lesson and last unit of work
- a knowledge organiser that is familiar to pupils, with sections blanked out
- drawing a diagram of a volcano from memory
- labelling a diagram of a river from memory
- identifying landmarks from around the UK from pictures
- writing definitions of key geographical terms.

Research from cognitive science explains that our memories have strength: both storage strength, as referred to in 'Spaced learning' above, and retrieval strength.

Retrieval strength refers to how readily available information is; if we can recall something, the retrieval strength is strong; if we struggle to remember something, then the retrieval strength is weaker. For primary pupils, this illustrates why it is important to quiz or ask them to think about things they've learned before: because doing so helps to improve their retrieval strength.

Using information from a retrieval task has the added benefit of revealing misconceptions or gaps in learning. This can help identify pupils who may need additional support or highlight content that may need to be retaught. Knowing that cognitive science supports the use of strategies for retrieval helps us as teachers to be confident that we are making a positive impact on learning.

4. Managing cognitive load

Building on the work of Baddeley and Hitch (Baddeley et al., 1974), in 1988, John Sweller coined the term 'cognitive load theory' (Sweller, 1988). The theory, in its simplest terms, is based on the idea that our working memory, where we temporarily hold the information we are thinking about, is limited.

Research shows that our working memory can hold around four pieces of information at any given time, and this is thought to be reduced in young children and the elderly (Cowan, 2001). After this point, information can be transferred from our working memory to our long-term memory, or it can be forgotten.

Our long-term memory stores our knowledge and memories. In contrast to our working memory, which has limited capacity, our long-term memory is unlimited (Baddeley, 2003). In a situation where there is too much information for our working memory to hold, it fails, and learning is much less effective. This is called 'cognitive overload.'

What might cognitive overload look like?

Gathercole and Alloway (2007) explain that when our working memory fails, we are cognitively overloaded, which may present in one or more of the following ways:

- incomplete recall
- failure to follow instructions (for example remembering part but not all of a sequence of instructions)
- place keeping errors (for example missing out words when writing a sentence)
- task abandonment (where a pupil just 'gives up' because a task appears too challenging).

Implications for the geography curriculum

Consider this example from a Key Stage 2 geography lesson:

Teacher: *'Today we are learning about South America. It is an interesting continent with lots of fascinating physical and human features. We will be using our atlases today. You need to find the contents page and work out which page the continent of South America is on. When you've done that, can you identify some of the countries in South America? Jack, can you just pull that blind down thanks. You may want to find some rivers and mountain ranges too. Lena, aren't there enough atlases? Go and ask Year 4 if they have any. After that you need to label your map, remember to use a sharp pencil, and make sure you use capital letters for country names. Who hasn't got an atlas now? Ok good off you go.'*

In this example you can see that there is a real risk of cognitive overload.

If we work with the theory that we can hold around four pieces of information in our working memories, pupils might be able to follow the first few things the teacher is saying: up to, 'When you've done that…' but after this point pupils are likely to be overloaded and therefore will not remember what they have been asked to do. Pupils with secure prior knowledge might cope better in this scenario, but those with little prior knowledge would be easily overwhelmed.

As teachers, we might often find ourselves repeating instructions endlessly, which can be frustrating, but it could be the case that pupils have simply been overloaded with information, cannot remember the sequence of instructions and therefore fail to follow them. It is the most vulnerable learners in our classrooms who will struggle the most when teaching does not consider cognitive load.

Understanding cognitive load theory and the resulting implications for teaching geography is vital to being able to support all pupils, particularly those who have less secure prior knowledge.

Strategies to avoid overloading working memory in the geography classroom

Gathercole and Alloway (2007) suggest the following strategies to avoid overloading working memory in the classroom:

- **Reduce load on working memory** – this can be achieved by considering how much pupils are expected to remember at a given time.

- **Increase the meaningfulness and familiarity of what is to be remembered** – you may like to consider pupils using the same atlas in each key stage. This would help them to become familiar with using it, reducing cognitive load and allowing them to focus on the geography content they are learning.

- **Simplifying verbal instructions** – this is important when pupils are using resources such as maps, data and atlases, as teachers need to be very clear about what pupils are expected to do.

- **Reducing processing demands** – as leaders, we can support staff to embed routines, for example, ensuring they have the correct number of atlases before the lesson, having designated partners for map work so pupils know who to share with.

- **Restructuring multistep tasks into separate independent steps, supported by memory aids** – when asking pupils to draw a map, which is a task with multiple steps, restructure this by modelling each step using a visualiser. Some pupils may benefit from having the key elements on their map as a tick list or within a word bank.

- **Making available and encouraging the use of memory aids** – you may like to promote the use of note-taking on whiteboards for older pupils, using maps or pictures as memory aids when pupils are writing.

Optimising cognitive load

The EEF review referred to at the start of this chapter explains that strategies within the classroom should aim to manage cognitive load, not to minimise it. We don't want to make our geography lessons too easy for pupils; we want them to be challenging and interesting, supporting learning over time. Managing, or optimising cognitive load requires us to think about *what* information is being taught and *how* it is being taught within our geography curriculum and within the lessons that deliver it.

Reflect on cognitive load within the classroom

If you have an opportunity to watch a colleague teaching geography, you may like to reflect on the following questions that focus on managing cognitive load within the classroom:

Reflection question	What you are looking for
1. Was new information broken down into manageable chunks?	**Consider** how clearly the teacher provided explanations. For example, when teaching map symbols, did the teacher introduce a few symbols at a time and ensure pupils could identify them before introducing more? **Reflect** on how engaged pupils were in the taught part of the lesson (for example through questioning, use of talk partners or mini whiteboards). For example, when teaching KS2 about biomes, did the teacher introduce a biome and ask pupils to discuss its features before moving on to the next one?
2. Were distractions minimised and resources organised?	**Consider** how the teachers minimised distractions, such as pupils moving around, during the taught part of the lesson. **Reflect** on how resources were prepared. For example, when introducing the countries of the UK, did the teacher have a clear map with no additional information that could confuse pupils. **Notice** what pupils are expected to focus on, for example slides on a whiteboard, maps, atlases, pictures or diagrams. For example, if a teacher uses a diagram of the water cycle, is it clear and free from clutter of additional information?
3. How does the teacher support working memory during the lesson?	**Consider** how the teacher revisits prior knowledge during the lesson. For example, when studying local geography, a teacher may show photos of a recent walk around the local area to remind pupils what they saw before moving on. **Reflect** on the use of diagrams and other memory aids, if applicable. **Notice** careful planning for managing cognitive load. For example, when a teacher explains an element of the water cycle, do they ask pupils to discuss what occurs using key vocabulary before they explain the next element?
4. How are all pupils supported to access the lesson?	**Notice** cognitive supports for pupils who need support, such as word banks, knowledge organisers, sentence stems, labelled diagrams and labelled maps.
5. How does the teacher make connections between new geographical concepts and existing knowledge to help optimise cognitive load?	**Notice** references to prior learning, such as showing pupils a previous knowledge organiser, showing some slides from previous lessons, asking pupils to discuss previously learned content. **Reflect** on how pupils are building on their prior knowledge. For example, a teacher might ask pupils to discuss the weather in England and their knowledge of the seasons before introducing the monsoon season in India.

5. Working with schemas

A schema is a structure that organises knowledge and understanding. We add to our existing schema each time we learn something new, connecting new knowledge with pre-existing schema.

Understanding this is important for primary teachers because we are always looking to develop pupils' knowledge and understanding. Therefore, it is helpful to consider where pupils' starting points are and what they already know, so we can understand where the new knowledge we are teaching will fit in with their existing schema.

Implications for the geography curriculum

Here is an example of adding new knowledge to an existing schema:

Encounter 1	Encounter 2	Encounter 3	Encounter 4
Volcanoes are cone shaped. They erupt, spewing out hot lava from the top of the cone.	A volcano is cone shaped and eruptions can continue for long periods of time. Gas, ash and lava can erupt from cracks in the surface of the volcano.	Not all volcanoes are cone shaped, some are shaped like shields; some are large cracks in the ground. Hot springs can be found near volcanoes.	Iceland is located on a tectonic plate boundary and there is a lot of volcanic activity there. Eruptions can create new land as lava flows into the sea and cools.

In this example, a pupil begins with an understanding of volcanoes, and their schema extends as far as classic cone-shaped volcanoes that erupt from the top of the cone. This is a good foundation from which to build their understanding. Each time the pupil encounters volcanoes again in their geography curriculum, they are adding to and extending their schema.

Of course, it is not possible to understand exactly what individual pupils' schemas will be like. They are not visible and are shaped by the experiences that each individual has had. However, despite this challenge, we can consider the content of the curriculum pupils have experienced and we can ensure it is designed to build on prior knowledge and extend understanding.

Schema building

The EEF report (Perry et al., 2021) suggests three ways that teachers can support schema building:

- concept/knowledge mapping
- schema/concept comparison and cognitive conflict
- elaboration and self-explanation.

Concept/knowledge mapping

Concept/knowledge mapping involves the creation of visual concept maps or knowledge organisers which allow pupils to see the key elements of their curriculum content and how they may connect.

At primary level, this may be done at a simple level, with one concept and some key connected information noted. It is helpful to keep knowledge organisers as simple as possible, including only the key information you want pupils to remember. The report explains that there is some evidence that these strategies support learning, but it suggests that there are challenges with implementation. The evidence indicates that the level of engagement a pupil has with their curriculum content is more important than any specific format for concept/knowledge mapping.

Schema/concept comparison and cognitive conflict

Schema/concept comparison and cognitive conflict requires pupils to consider two concepts at the same time and to compare and contrast them, leading to a clearer understanding.

Implications for the geography curriculum

In some cases in primary geography it might be useful to consider concept comparison and cognitive conflict when there are two related concepts that may confuse pupils. Here is an example of concept comparison:

In practice: concept comparison

Pre-existing schema	Weather – pupils can identify different types of weather including rain, sun, wind, snow.
New knowledge	Climate – pupils learn that climate describes the patterns of weather over a long period of time in a certain place. They may learn that the climate in the Mediterranean is warm and dry in the summers but can, on occasions, be wet.

In this example, pupils are grappling with two concepts: climate and weather. By thinking about these two things at the same time, they refine their understanding and over time can understand the difference between the two.

In practice: cognitive conflict

Here is an example of a cognitive conflict:

Pre-existing schema	Pupils could think that a river runs in a straight line from its source to the sea.
Conflicting information	Pupils learn that rivers can change course or meander and that they can change in depth, width, speed of flow (velocity) and the slope of the land.

In this example, pupils learn that rivers change over their course and can look and move differently at different points. This cognitive conflict adjusts understanding, encouraging deeper learning as pupils learn and understand more.

Both examples show ways to support pupils' understanding of geographical concepts. Understanding the cognitive processes occurring when these strategies are implemented helps us to select the appropriate time to use them within our geography curriculum.

Elaboration and self-explanation

The EEF report mentions elaboration and self-explanation as strategies that teachers may use to support schema building.

- **Elaboration** means adding detail, such as asking a pupils to build on a response or asking pupils what else they know about a given element within the curriculum.
- **Self-explanation** requires pupils to explain a concept or geographical process in their own words.

Although the report explains that evidence for these strategies is currently very limited, asking pupils to explain or add detail to an explanation will require them to think carefully about the content of the curriculum and therefore, we can expect a positive impact on learning.

Implications for the geography curriculum

In practice: elaboration

Teacher:	'The River Thames is an important river in England.' 'Talk to your partner. Could we add more detail to this statement?'
Partner discussion. (Teacher can hear pupils talking about the benefits of rivers to cities including transport, trade and water for agriculture.)	
Pupil 1:	'We talked about cities growing up around rivers, because people need water to grow crops, like in Ancient Egypt. In England, the city of London was built near the Thames because people could use the water for the things they needed and for their ships to trade.'
Pupil 2:	'Rivers are also important for animals, for fish and other wildlife, for their habitats.'

In this example, pupils have made connections with their history knowledge and are applying it to this question in a geography lesson. They have also made a connection with science and their understanding of animals and habitats.

This opportunity to elaborate helps pupils to deepen their knowledge and understanding.

---

6. Multimedia learning

Multimedia learning refers to the use of more than one medium for delivering learning, such as the combination of audio and visual materials. For example, a teacher could use a map as a visual support for pupils whilst explaining the key features of the map. In this scenario, pupils are listening and looking at the map at the same time.

This approach is thought to support effective learning. It is based on the understanding that our working memory has both a visual and an auditory component. By engaging both, we can support learning without overloading working memory.

Implications for the geography curriculum

When you think about using multimedia within geography lessons, it is useful to consider what pupils are seeing and listening to. If the information is not presented clearly, or if there is lots of extra information, then effective learning will be harder for them.

Audio and visual materials from quality sources such as BBC Bitesize or National Geographic Kids are useful to use in the classroom and tend to be very clear as they are designed for young learners.

It is useful for geography leaders to have oversight of what resources teachers are using so they can ensure they are clear and of high quality.

The EEF report (Perry et al., 2021) explains that there is no clear evidence of precise multimedia learning strategies, but teachers should consider how and when they use images and auditory resources in their lessons clearly and purposefully.

Some examples of multimedia learning in geography:

- exploring maps (for example displaying a map and explaining key features of the map)

- drawing and narrating diagrams (for example drawing a diagram of a rainforest on the whiteboard and narrating each addition to the diagram building up from the ground and explaining each layer)
- using interactive maps to explore different geographical locations
- using simple and clear images or icons when introducing new vocabulary.

7. Embodied learning

Embodied learning refers to learning strategies that make use of movement, for example asking pupils to make a mountain shape with their arms when introducing mountains in a geography lesson.

Physical movement during lessons will be familiar to many primary school teachers, particularly those in EYFS and Key Stage 1. When working with young pupils we often incorporate songs, actions, rhymes and movement into our teaching. Strategies such as these are thought to support memory and learning as it is understood that memory is closely related to the experience of our bodies (Madan et al., 2012).

Implications for the geography curriculum

Primary geography already maximises on the principles of embodied learning as pupils are taken out of the classroom to do fieldwork. The very essence of fieldwork, of hands-on learning, will support pupils' understanding as they engage in it. They will remember about the gradient of hills when they scramble up a steep hill; they will understand how water flows in a river that they've paddled in; they will see firsthand the impact of erosion when they stand on a beach at the foot of a cliff.

Using embodied learning in the classroom in geography could include:

- using actions for key words such as 'mountain', 'volcano', 'earthquake'
- asking pupils to use their arms like a needle in a compass to show direction
- role playing a meteorologist giving a weather report.

In practice: using embodied learning in the classroom

	EYFS	KS1	KS2
Outside the classroom	Go for a walk around the school grounds and look closely at what is growing, for example trees and plants.	Go for a walk around the local area and look closely at the areas of green space. Encourage pupils to think about what they see, hear and feel in different locations.	Visit a contrasting environment, for example a rural area if your school is located in a city. Find out what pupils notice about how the landscape is different from their local area.
Inside the classroom	Use actions to teach words such as 'mountain' and 'river' when pupils come across them in stories and songs.	Use actions to teach the four points of a compass and ask pupils to point to North, South, East and West.	Use drama to write and perform a weather report based on knowledge of meteorology. Have a map of the region pupils are reporting on to refer to.

It is important to highlight that when applying cognitive science principles to a classroom context, you are interpreting research and suggesting strategies that may have not been applied in the context within which you work. Sometimes, strategies may work in one classroom, but for a variety of reasons they may not work in another.

We know that teaching is not an exact science! However, understanding findings from cognitive science can inform our practice. We can consider when, why and how strategies could apply to our classroom context. Importantly, aspects of cognitive science can be considered together, enabling us to have conversations about curriculum and pedagogy that focus on improving pupil outcomes.

Case study: engaging with cognitive science research

Kate is a geography subject lead at a one form entry primary school in Luton.

She has recently learned about cognitive science as part of her Early Career Teacher (ECT) course.

Although her school has a well-established geography curriculum, she would like to introduce some strategies suggested by cognitive science to support pupils' learning and memory.

During her leadership time, Kate undertakes some pupil voice, where she asks three pupils from each year group about their geography lessons and writes down some of their responses. She wants to find out what they are remembering from the geography curriculum. She asks the pupils about some of the key geography content from their current year and from previous years. It reveals that many of the pupils are not retaining knowledge from previous years and are finding it hard to transfer knowledge to unfamiliar contexts.

Kate shares her concerns with her ECT mentor and talks to some of the other teachers in the school. They agree that while the curriculum seems well sequenced, pupils don't remember as much of the curriculum as teachers would like. Teachers do retrieval tasks but they tend to focus on what pupils did in the previous lesson and don't go further back, so pupils lack opportunities to revisit content from previous topics or years. They often report there is a lot of content to 'get through.'

Kate would like teachers to understand cognitive load theory. She would like teachers to feel confident in breaking down their geography teaching into small, manageable chunks. She would also like teachers to utilise strategies that support learning and memory, such as spaced retrieval.

In the short term, she prioritises making a tweak to the lesson structure of geography lessons so that they include spaced retrieval of previous units as part of a starter activity.

She plans two professional development sessions for teachers to support this. One session will be on cognitive load theory and how teachers can manage cognitive load within geography lessons and break material down into manageable chunks. The second session will focus on how to plan and deliver the new spaced retrieval part of the lesson, with opportunities for teachers to practise with their peers.

Chapter summary

In this chapter we have looked at the EEF's report on cognitive science and its application in the classroom. We explored the following areas and considered the implications for primary geography:

- Spaced learning (when content is taught) – how your geography curriculum is designed and sequenced and how you structure your individual geography lessons to ensure pupils revisit content and remember it.

- Interleaving (the practice of switching between different but related types of problems or ideas within the same lesson or learning period) – for example, planning retrieval quizzes to give pupils an opportunity to remember content from previous topics.

- Retrieval practice (asking pupils to remember previously taught content) – helping them to remember it over time and revealing misconceptions or gaps in learning.

- Managing cognitive load – requires you to think about *what* information is being taught and *how* it is being taught within your geography curriculum and within the lessons that deliver it.

- Working with schemas (a structure that organises knowledge and understanding) – helps to place new learning in a context of what pupils already understand in geography, supporting their overall understanding.

- Multimedia learning (the use of more than one medium for delivering learning, such as the combination of audio and visual materials) – for example, using a map or pictures and talking to explain at the same time.

- Embodied learning (learning strategies that make use of movement) – for example, to support understanding when we introduce new vocabulary.

Questions for reflection

- How does our geography curriculum enable spaced learning?
- How do our geography lessons incorporate retrieval practice?
- How do our pupils build schemas in geography from EYFS to Key Stage 2?

Example PD session: optimising cognitive load

Here is an example of what a PD session on optimising cognitive load could look like.

TIMING SUGGESTION	SESSION GUIDANCE
10 mins	Share an article about cognitive load theory with staff, for example: 'Cognitive load theory and its application in the classroom' (Shibli and West, 2018).
5 mins	Ask teachers to respond to the article and share their thoughts with colleagues. Reflect on how findings from cognitive science might inform our classroom practice.
15 mins	Discuss suggested strategies based on cognitive science, such as managing cognitive load by breaking information down into small manageable chunks or spaced retrieval practice. What might this look like across the school from EYFS to KS2?
20 mins	Give teachers the opportunity to look at their forthcoming geography lessons and plan how they will manage cognitive load during the lesson. Teachers could decide where it is most effective to add in opportunities for spaced retrieval practice.

Explore further

- *Cognitive Science Approaches in the Classroom: a review of the evidence* (2021) by Perry et al.
- *Understanding How we Learn* (2019) by Yana Weinstein and Megan Sumeracki
- 'Cognitive load theory and its application in the classroom' (2018) by Dominic Shibli and Rachel West
- *How Learning Happens: Seminal Works in Educational Psychology and What They Mean in Practice* (2020) by Paul Kirschner and Carl Hendrick
- 'Interweaving Geography' in *Teaching Geography*, Spring 2020, Vol. 45, No. 1 by Mark Enser

4 Developing a sense of place, space and belonging

Geography has a central role in young children's developing identity. As we considered in Chapter 1, young children are likely to be asking challenging questions of themselves as they grow, such as: *Where am I? Where can I go? Where do I belong?* Throughout their childhood, the pupils you teach will construct ideas of place and space and make connections between their own experiences and the world they live in. You can support this growing understanding with your geography curriculum. By teaching geography and supporting pupils' understanding of the world around them, we can help them establish their own identity and a sense of belonging.

This chapter will explore:

- place and space as concepts – and their importance in geography
- how to support pupils' understanding of place within the primary curriculum
- developing a sense of belonging.

Place and space as concepts

Place

As primary geography leaders, it is helpful for us to understand some of the important concepts that form the substance of our subject. Place is a hugely important concept within geography, and its meaning has been discussed, theorised and developed for many, many years.

The Greek Philosopher Aristotle (384–322 BC) valued place, saying it 'takes precedence over all things' (Casey, 1997, p.52). He considered place the starting point from which we can understand more about the world, because everything exists somewhere. From this, we can understand that place has a specific meaning: it is about an actual location and what occurs in that location.

However, what seems like a concept that is straightforward to define is actually much more challenging. A place can be where we live, a place where we go to work, 'the workplace', our favourite restaurant, the place we go to watch our favourite football team play. We also talk about our 'place' within a family and friendship group. On a larger scale, a place could be a town or city; it could be a country, the place our country has on a global stage. There has been much debate over the UK's place in the European Union in recent years. As Tim Cresswell identifies, 'Place, then, is not scale specific. It can be as small as a setting at a table and as large as the Earth' (Cresswell, 2008, p. 134).

Although there is no simple definition of place, as geography leaders, it is important to understand this concept and what it means to the primary-aged pupils we teach. When geographers describe places, they ask: *Where is this place? What is in this place? Why it is here? How is this place changing?* They may look at a place's physical and human geography, considering how the two are connected and interact. There is an important locational aspect to place, but meaning can be found beyond the locational information. 'Places are locations with meaning' (Cresswell, 2008, p. 134). This is a good starting point for primary geography as it focuses pupils' attention on the location and features of a place, which, over time, will create a foundational understanding of the diversity of places in the locality, the country and the wider world.

'Place is primary because it is the experiential fact of our existence' (Cresswell, 2014, p. 50). For the pupils we teach, the concept of place will relate directly to their understanding and experience of their surroundings. Pupils may be experiencing places for the first time as they move through their primary education, both in and out of school. Perhaps their first trip to a beach, their first journey on a coach, their first exploration through a forest, their first paddle in a river. These experiences will play an important role in their developing sense of place.

As geography leaders, we can look at our curriculum and ask ourselves, 'How does our curriculum help to develop a child's understanding of place?' We can also reflect on our place in the context of our school. What is the place like that we educate our pupils within? How are pupils shaped by the place they learn and how do they shape the place they learn in?

Space

As with place, there is no straightforward way of defining the concept of space. Geographers have long debated the meaning of space and will continue to do so as our world changes. Our spatial awareness relates to where we are within a given space and recognition of what is around us. Our spatial sense is our understanding of position, direction, movement and location.

In geography, we ask pupils to locate places, which in turn develops a sense of space as they ponder, 'Where is this city/river/mountain/continent located? Is it near to me? Is it far from where I am?' As pupils journey through the curriculum, they will develop a sense of space as they learn more about locations around the world and discover what is near, what is far away and what comes in between. This developing sense of space will be supported by understanding how geographers divide the world using imaginary lines (for example: lines of longitude and latitude, the equator, and the tropics), in order to make spatial sense of the world.

For primary geography, it is helpful to consider how pupils' understanding of space grows over time as they become more familiar with the world around them. It is not, however, a specific requirement of the National Curriculum in England, which identifies location knowledge, place knowledge, human and physical geography and geographical skills and fieldwork as areas of study (DfE, 2013).

As primary geography leaders, we can focus on place within the curriculum but also remember that pupils will be developing a sense of space. In primary schools we are laying the foundations for future learning; an individual's understanding of both place and space will continue to grow and change well into adulthood as they continue to learn, experience and make meaning in the world around them.

How to support pupils' understanding of place within the primary curriculum

As a primary geography leader, it is useful to work with the understanding that 'place' as a concept adds meaning to a specific location, giving it context. When we consider our place knowledge, it is the 'what' we know about a place: is it in a city? Does it have a river? What grows there? What jobs do people do? Is it warm? Does it rain a lot? Within our primary curriculum, we offer opportunities for pupils to learn about their local area and familiarise themselves with local geographical features. They will gain place knowledge and will be developing a sense of identity as they learn about the place in which they live.

Some pupils will have well-established connections to a place. They will come to school knowing where they are and they will be familiar with local places as they will have had experiences there, such as going to a local park, a swimming pool or a supermarket. Other pupils may not have these connections. They may have just moved to an area or they may not have had the same early childhood experiences as others. Through our geography curriculum, we can ensure that all pupils, regardless of prior experience, are afforded opportunities to connect with their local area and the world around them through curriculum content and fieldwork opportunities.

Early Years Foundation Stage (EYFS)

Understanding geographical similarities and differences is an important aspect of place knowledge within the curriculum. The journey your pupils will go on in geography begins in EYFS. It is important for leaders of geography to understand what geography looks like for your youngest learners and how it is woven through the curriculum.

In EYFS, pupils learn about their immediate environment and know some similarities and differences between life in this country and life in other countries. This is described below in the Early Learning Goal: People, Culture and Communities (one of three Early Learning Goals within the area of learning called 'Understanding the World'):

> 'Children at the expected level of development will:
>
> • Describe their immediate environment using knowledge from observation, discussion, stories, non-fiction texts, and maps.
> • Know some similarities and differences between different religious and cultural communities in this country, drawing on their experiences and what has been read in class.
> • Explain some similarities and differences between life in this country and life in other countries, drawing on knowledge from stories, non-fiction texts and – when appropriate – maps.'
>
> (Early Years Statutory Framework, 2014, p. 15)

As a geography leader, we will not be able to observe geography lessons in EYFS but we can look for ways in which our youngest pupils are developing their geographical thinking. We may identify activities such as these that support early geographical understanding:

• Pupils go on a walk around the perimeter of the school grounds or into the immediate area around the school. Teachers may have taught some key vocabulary prior to this walk that they will use in context, such as place names or feature names.

- When outside of the classroom, pupils might take clipboards to draw simple maps and/or digital cameras to take photographs. They might identify some key places in their local area such as a park or shops.
- Pupils might be able to talk about their journey to school and what they pass on the way.
- Pupils might use photos to annotate a map of the local area. They might continue to draw maps or routes that are familiar to them.
- Pupils could use tools such as programmable floor robots to begin to understand direction and position. Activities such as this support their understanding of their local area and what is located there.

National Curriculum Key Stages 1 and 2

Following on from EYFS, the National Curriculum in England specifies the progression of place knowledge in Key Stages 1 and 2 in the following way:

Geographical similarities and differences	KS1	• A small area of the United Kingdom • A small area in a contrasting non-European country	For example: a study of Lyme Regis in the South of England and its location along the Jurassic coastline For example: a study of San Francisco, its grid formation and the peninsula it is located on
	KS2	• A region of the United Kingdom • A region in a European Country • A region within North or South America	For example: a study of the Lake District and its physical features For example: the Alps and their location in Europe For example: the Amazon rainforest in South America and the challenges of the region

The National Curriculum in England does not identify the difference between a small area and a region. However, we can assume that a small area might mean a single city, a town, or a geographical area of a few miles, whereas a region could be a more extensive area encompassing several towns and cities.

When pupils study different places across their geography curriculum, they will understand what geographers look for and the questions they may ask. They will identify similarities and differences between the place they are studying and those they have previously studied. This foundational place knowledge will support their future learning, enabling them to connect to places worldwide.

In practice: a study of a small area of the United Kingdom - Lyme Regis, Key Stage 1

Location: South coast of England

Enquiry question: What is interesting about Lyme Regis?

Lesson 1: Share the enquiry question: What is interesting about Lyme Regis? Explain what we will learn about this place in order to answer the question. Show the location of Lyme Regis on the Jurassic Coastline in England (building on prior UK knowledge).

Lesson 2: Map work identifying key locations, such as harbour and museum, on a map.

Lesson 3: Explore Lyme Regis' physical features: cliffs, beaches and fossil-rich coast, building on map work from lesson 2.

Lesson 4: Explore Lyme Regis' human features, for example the harbour, shops, cafes and museum, and tourism and its importance in the town – building on map work from lessons 2 and 3.

Lesson 5: Learn about the Jurassic coastline; understanding its history and importance of geology.

Lesson 6: Answer the enquiry question: what is interesting about Lyme Regis? This piece of extended writing could include maps and pictures.

In practice: a study of a region in a European country - south coast of France, Key Stage 2

Enquiry question: How does the geography of the south coast of France affect people who live there?

Lesson 1: Share the enquiry question: How does the geography of the south coast of France affect people who live there? Explain that we will be learning about the south coast of France and looking for answers to this question. Locational knowledge: Nice, Marseilles, Saint-Tropez, the Alps, Mediterranean Sea – using maps to identify key places.

Lesson 2: Compare and contrast the climate of Grenoble (in the Alps) and Nice (on the coastline) using temperature and rainfall data.

Lesson 3: Explore the human geography of the region, including economic activity and population density, locating cities such as Marseille and using population maps to identify areas of dense and sparse population.

Lesson 4: Tourism: find out why people come to the region, for example beaches, vineyards, ski resorts, and look at images of the region.

Lesson 5: Compare and contrast the south coast of France with a region of the UK, for example the Lake District, exploring climate, population, and landscape using data and knowledge of the regions.

Lesson 6: Answer the enquiry question: how does the geography of the south coast of France affect people who live there? Use data and knowledge from previous lessons.

The curriculum content has been carefully planned in the two examples to develop pupils' place knowledge over time. Each lesson builds on the previous lesson and contributes to the enquiry question, which pupils will answer at the end of the unit. The place knowledge has been broken down into manageable chunks with opportunities to engage with map work in both key stages and data in Key Stage 2. The two units require pupils to look at a stretch of coastline, one in England and the other in France. This will support their place knowledge as they recognise similarities and differences between the two areas/regions.

Developing a sense of belonging

Physical geography studies the natural environment; human geography studies the relationship between humans and the natural environment. It asks questions such as: *What do we do in this place? How have we changed it? How has it shaped how we live? Will it always remain the same?* We have established the importance of developing a sense of place for young children, and establishing place knowledge helps them compare and contrast places, making connections. However, place knowledge does more than layer knowledge of places for our pupils, it helps to develop their sense of belonging.

'A sense of belonging contributes to children's overall social and emotional development and is an essential aspect of school readiness' (Epstein, 2009).

What do we mean by belonging? Belonging has multiple meanings but also has a strong connection to geography. 'Belonging connects matter to place, through various practices of boundary making and inhabitation which signal that a particular collection of objects, animals, plants, germs, people, practices, performances, or ideas is meant `to be' in a place' (Mee et al., 2009). Geographical research in recent years has reflected upon the concept of belonging in light of the movement, sometimes forced, of people worldwide.

When we teach young pupils geography, we simplify the world around us so that they can understand it. So, for many young pupils, the concept of a country border is definitive: this is where one country is; across the border is another country. This is a good place to start for pupils, but as they get older and learn more about the world, they will see that sometimes borders change, or that borders can be areas of conflict.

For other pupils, their early life experiences might have left them questioning where they belong; they might be in education in a place where they do not feel they belong. As a geography leader, knowing the school community well will help you to shape the curriculum so that it can support all pupils and include their experiences. If you have refugee children within your school community, it may be helpful to discuss your curriculum with senior leaders to ensure their needs and experiences are considered.

Our primary geography curriculum has a responsibility to deliver the knowledge and experiences pupils need to develop their own sense of identity and belonging. Through carefully choosing of the content in our geography curriculum, we can ensure pupils have encountered important places and processes around the world that will shape their understanding.

For example, pupils could:

- Engage with their local area – leaders should identify key places in the local area that could contribute to pupils' geographical understanding, such as a local river, local green spaces, coastline or other physical features. Pupils can think about how these features are managed and how humans interact with them. This will help them to develop a sense of connection and recognise the responsibility we all have to be stewards of our local area.

- Learn about countries or regions in the world that are connected to the school population – for example, some schools will have welcomed children from Ukraine in recent years. Geography leaders can look at where there are opportunities to include Eastern European geography in their curriculum, in order for pupils to feel included and to learn about places they are connected to.

Our geography curriculum can reveal the world to pupils and help them understand where they are, what is around them, and what is out there for them to discover as they learn and grow.

Case study: developing a sense of belonging, Cavendish Primary School, London

At Cavendish Primary School, our values of belonging, kindness, curiosity, confidence and ambition permeate every aspect of school life. We believe that a sense of belonging is essential to nurturing positive relationships, fostering self-worth and enabling successful learning.

Our geography curriculum plays a pivotal role in delivering our values, as pupils learn about themselves and their place in our community and the wider world.

Located in west London, just a few minutes' stroll to the River Thames and backing onto the conservation area of Dukes Meadows Trust, our school has a unique locality offering a rich geographical experience and many opportunities for fieldwork. Through our geography curriculum, our pupils develop a deep understanding of the sense of place. They learn about and explore the local area from EYFS to Year Six and make connections to the world as they acquire knowledge and understanding.

Community partnerships provide valued opportunities for pupils' personal development linked to our locality, including ongoing work with

Chiswick House and Gardens, the RNLI and even the local allotments. We partner with Time Givers, a charity that provides opportunities to give back to our local community through volunteering in environmental activities and connecting with people within our community, including senior citizens. These experiences offer valued opportunities to connect with others and our locality.

Combining the curriculum with carefully planned personal development, based on our unique location, ensures that all pupils, no matter their background, have a good understanding of the world. This helps our children to recognise that they are valued citizens within our community and beyond.

Importantly, for our staff and children, a genuine sense of belonging brings the opportunity to thrive as learners and citizens. They can be confident in who they are as individuals, and have the knowledge and curiosity to connect with people and the world they live in.

Chapter summary

In this chapter we have considered the following:

- As a geography leader, you need to understand what place and space mean to young pupils.
- You might like to consider how place knowledge develops within the National Curriculum in England or your national curriculum.
- It might be helpful to explore how understanding place and space can be linked to belonging.
- You might want some further discussion with school leaders on how the value of belonging can have an important role within the primary geography curriculum.

Questions for reflection

- Which places do our children learn about?
- What does the sequence of place knowledge look like?

- Does the study of each chosen place within our curriculum build on prior learning?
- How does place knowledge within the curriculum relate to our pupils' experiences?
- How does our geography curriculum offer opportunities for pupils to develop connections to the places they study?
- How does our geography curriculum foster a sense of belonging for the pupils in our school?

Example PD session: developing place knowledge

Here is an example of what a PD session on developing place knowledge could look like.

TIMING SUGGESTION	SESSION GUIDANCE
10 mins	Discuss this excerpt from 'Getting our bearings' (Ofsted, 2023): 'Sometimes the resources that teachers have selected present an outdated and inaccurate view of the places being studied. At other times, pupils' knowledge of places is little more than a list of disconnected facts. This often happens when pupils are expected to find out information for themselves, with little explicit teaching on how to organise this information into a coherent geographical understanding of the place.'
5 mins	Ask teachers to reflect on the places they teach and what pupils learn about these places.
15 mins	Look at the lesson sequence for a relevant unit focusing on place knowledge. What do pupils learn about that place? How does place knowledge connect to their prior learning? Are generalisations made and how accurate are these? How will pupils build on this place knowledge in the future?
20 mins	Give teachers the opportunity to look at place knowledge in their forthcoming geography units and consider how knowledge is developing effectively. How is place knowledge building on prior learning? How is the content of the curriculum connected and how do pupils build a strong understanding of place over time? Which places do pupils learn about in EYFS, KS1 and KS2? Which different kinds of places are pupils encountering, for example villages, towns, cities, rural areas? What connections can pupils make between places?

Explore further

- The Geographical Association's 'Place in geography': https://geography.org. uk/ite/initial-teacher-education/geography-support-for-trainees-and-ects/ learning-to-teach-secondary-geography/geography-subject-teaching-and-curriculum/geography-knowledge-concepts-and-skills/place-and-places/ place-in-geography/

- The Geographical Association's 'Teaching place knowledge': https://geogra phy.org.uk/ite/initial-teacher-education/geography-support-for-train ees-and-ects/learning-to-teach-secondary-geography/geography-subj ect-teaching-and-curriculum/geography-knowledge-concepts-and-skills/ place-and-places/teaching-place-knowledge/

The two resources above are written for secondary teachers but are both very useful for primary geography leads.

- This blog is helpful for some considerations before you teach a place: https://decolonisegeography.com/blog/2021/04/teaching-about-a-place-stop-and-think-first/.

5 Curriculum design

This chapter will explore some key considerations within primary geography curriculum design. We will look at curriculum choices (what content you choose to teach), structure (how you put the curriculum together) and sequencing (the order of your curriculum content). There will be key questions for you as a subject leader to consider when you are reflecting on your curriculum offer. We will suggest ways in which you can critique your current curriculum to ensure it is working well for the children in your school.

Curriculum design is complex and there are many different approaches. No two primary schools will have an identical geography curriculum, not least because our localities are not the same. However, there is common content within the curriculum that geography leaders in many different contexts can design thoughtfully to support their pupils' learning. This chapter will consider how to approach this. As Alex Standish, Associate Professor of Geography Education at UCL, points out, 'If you want to teach a subject you need to be able to clearly communicate to pupils what your subject is about and how it can help them to understand an aspect of the world' (Cuthbert et al., 2021, p. 137).

As pupils journey through the primary geography curriculum we want them to encounter opportunities to ask and answer geographical questions such as: *Where am I? What is around me? Why is this here?* Our curriculum design work should focus on revealing to pupils what geography is and what it can tell us about the world around us.

Many schools will purchase schemes of work to support their curriculum design and delivery; others may use a curriculum they have developed using expertise within their school. Whichever way your geography curriculum has been created, it is vital for you as a subject leader to understand the content, structure and sequence of the curriculum. Your geography curriculum must serve the pupils in your school, supporting their understanding over time. We will explore these elements of geography curriculum design in this chapter.

In this chapter, we will cover the following points:

- curriculum design principles
- EYFS curriculum and lesson structure
- Key Stages 1 and 2 curriculum content and structure.

Curriculum design principles

When considering curriculum design, we need to think about content choices, and structure and sequence.

Content choices

In geography, making content choices is about choosing the places, processes, geographical features and fieldwork that pupils will encounter before structuring and sequencing that content. Some places are specified in the National Curriculum in England, but we also have many decisions to make for ourselves in our own contexts. For example, the National Curriculum in England requires that pupils learn about a small area of the United Kingdom and a small area of a contrasting non-European country (DfE, 2013). Should we choose Birmingham and contrast it with San Francisco? Should we compare a city with a rural area? Do other areas of the curriculum link well to a location that we could choose?

These are all considerations for anyone thinking about curriculum design. We must choose which areas our children will learn about and identify what they will learn about those places and why. It is helpful to have a rationale that explains our decision making, as this will ensure the choices that have been made when designing the curriculum are understood by staff.

Structure and sequence

The structure of your geography curriculum is the way in which it has been planned. For example; local geography, UK geography, world geography. Within the structure of your geography curriculum, content will be sequenced, put into a logical order. For example, pupils will learn about aerial views before they look at maps.

The structure and sequence of your curriculum can, if planned well, create a systematic approach to learning primary geography. Ausubel (1968, p. vi) explained that 'the most important single factor influencing learning is what the learner already knows. Ascertain this and teach them accordingly.'

In a well-structured and specific curriculum, it is possible to identify what pupils should know and to then check if they know it before moving on to new content. Sequencing the content you have chosen requires careful consideration as to the order in which content should be introduced to ensure effective learning. For geography, this helps you to consider how pupils make progress across the subject, for example how they progress within fieldwork or map work or how their knowledge of human and physical features grows over time.

In practice: example of structure and sequence in action

'We have four main areas in our geography curriculum: local geography, UK geography, world geography and fieldwork. In each year group we make sure there is at least one opportunity for pupils to build knowledge and experiences within these areas. This is the overall structure of our curriculum. Then, within this structure, we can sequence content, meaning we put it in order. This helps us to plan for progression and we can ensure pupils build on their knowledge over time.

Fieldwork gets harder in each year group as pupils master skills such as reading an OS map, reading symbols using a key and identifying locations using grid references or co-ordinates. The structure and sequence of our geography curriculum is important because it creates a narrative for the subject; we know where pupils are on their journey, where they have been and where they are going next.'

These curriculum design principles can help to create a curriculum, but they also provide a framework from which teachers and leaders can assess the strength of their own curriculum. You might want to look at your curriculum and ask yourself the following questions:

- Which places do we choose to study and why?
- How is our curriculum structured?
- What order do pupils learn things in?

EYFS curriculum and lesson structure

For your youngest pupils, their introduction to geography has started long before they started school. Babies learn to navigate their immediate area when they begin to crawl. They interact with the world around them through touch, sound, smell and taste. Young children can begin to recognise familiar places, perhaps their grandparent's home, a supermarket or a local park.

Geography features in the EYFS framework for our pupils in Nursery and Reception. It is important for geography leaders to understand how this framework creates a foundation for future learning and how early geographical understanding starts to develop through play and exploration.

How geography is embedded in the seven areas of learning in the EYFS

Prime areas

- communication and language
- personal, social and emotional development
- physical development

These areas group fundamental aspects of early child development and each area supports development in the others. As pupils develop language and learn to communicate, they may begin to describe the world around them, talk about visible changes in the world around them such as leaves falling from the trees. They may describe places they have been that are important in their lives, such as visiting their grandparents or going to the park.

In their early years, children will be learning to physically navigate the world around them, which leads to interaction with others and in turn, helps to build both confidence and relationships. The curriculum and learning environment in EYFS should be designed to support development in these vital areas. The prime areas of learning form a strong foundation for future learning, and each will contribute to pupils' overall geographical understanding as they enter Key Stage 1.

Specific areas

- literacy
- mathematics
- understanding the world
- expressive arts and design

These areas of learning in EYFS introduce pupils to the knowledge and skills they need to engage with the world around them and thrive in their education. As they move through their geography education, the subject will require pupils to read, write, gather and interpret data and think creatively about solutions to geographical issues.

All of these areas of learning in EYFS contribute foundational knowledge and experiences for pupils that will support their future learning in geography and in the wider curriculum.

Geography is not taught as a discrete lesson in EYFS but is woven through the areas of learning and features particularly in 'understanding the world'. Within this area of learning, pupils have a specific goal to meet at the end of Reception: 'People, Culture and Communities.' As geography leader, it is helpful to talk to the EYFS leader about how pupils achieve this goal.

Your youngest pupils will be encountering their local area and the wider world within the EYFS curriculum as a whole. They will be listening to stories, hearing and saying new words, looking at pictures, engaging with maps, communicating with peers and adults, whilst also learning how to physically navigate their immediate environment through play and exploration.

Although the EYFS curriculum looks very different to the curriculum in Key Stages 1 and 2, it is important to identify how the curriculum is forming the foundations for future geographical understanding. In terms of curriculum design and understanding how pupils' geographical understanding builds over time, you can explore the following question as a thread for curriculum conversations with colleagues.

In practice: which places will pupils encounter within the EYFS curriculum?

'The EYFS framework allows us to choose which places our pupils learn about.

In our school, pupils learn about their local area in the first term of Reception. They learn where our school is located and about the town we live in. We use an aerial photograph. They look at a map of the local area and we locate the school.

We have a large map of the world displayed in our classroom and we label places that mean something to the pupils, for example where their families are from and where they have been on holiday. In the Spring term, we learn all about transport around the world. We have a globe for pupils to explore. We share stories, videos and pictures featuring different types of transport and we locate countries such as Thailand and Japan. We also learn about animals who live in cold places and we use the globe to show pupils where the North and South Poles are located.

In the Summer term, we have a world food celebration in school. In Reception we make pizzas and show pupils where Italy is on a map. We also use maps to locate places around the world that pupils are interested in. For example, some of our pupils love football and are interested in where the World Cup teams are from.'

In this example, pupils in Reception begin learning about their local area. This helps them to make connections with the places they see in their everyday lives and builds on their understanding from their pre-school years. Places that are important to your pupils can be incorporated into the curriculum here; perhaps a local park that is familiar to them or shops or local landmarks they might recognise. Pupils will go on to study their local area in more depth in Key Stage 1 and will continue to build on this knowledge into Key Stage 2.

Also in this example, pupils learn about some places around the world. Their understanding of scale is only beginning to develop at this stage in their geography education and may be limited to an understanding of 'near and far' depending on their experiences. As pupils are introduced to places around the world, they can begin to form a mental model of the globe, developing their locational and place knowledge over time as they progress through their schooling. This introduction to the wider world in EYFS will foster curiosity as pupils start to wonder what else is out there in the world. When leading geography in primary schools, it is useful to know which places your pupils learn about in EYFS and how the subsequent curriculum builds on this strong foundation.

Key Stages 1 and 2 curriculum content and structure

Key Stage 1

In Key Stage 1, pupils will learn more about their own locality, the UK and the wider world. They will begin to use geographical skills, for example using maps and compasses to develop locational awareness. As leaders, it is important for us to understand how our Key Stage 1 curriculum is designed to build on from the foundation of EYFS. We also need to know how and when our curriculum introduces new geography content, how it is structured and sequenced. We will explore an example of how geography content is introduced below.

In practice: when is the geography of the UK introduced in the curriculum and what do pupils learn?

'In Year 1, pupils study a unit of work on the UK. They learn about the four countries of the UK and their capital cities. They learn about some of the characteristics of the countries in the UK such as the Welsh valleys and the Scottish lochs. They use atlases

to look at maps of the UK and its surrounding seas. We introduce the four-point compass here and use directional language to describe the location of key features on a map.

Following this, in Year 2, pupils build on this knowledge and learn more about the UK. They develop place knowledge by studying a small area of the UK. We study our local area here (an area of West London) and then we contrast it with San Francisco. Pupils look at geographical similarities and differences in both the physical and human geography of the area. They contrast the locations: London being inland located along a river and San Francisco being located on a peninsula. They contrast the transportation: London offering buses, trains and underground trains and San Francisco offering buses and trams and a small underground network and bridges. They contrast the Golden Gate Bridge in San Francisco and Hammersmith bridge in London. This knowledge of the UK from Key Stage 1 is built upon in Year 2 when they study a unit that looks at geographical issues in the UK such as flooding, air pollution and waste management.'

In this example, it is possible to identify when pupils begin to learn about the UK, what they learn and how that builds into the curriculum in Year 2. This approach to curriculum design ensures that pupils are learning and remembering more over time, building on their prior knowledge. When pupils move to Key Stage 2 they have a strong foundation of knowledge of the geography of the United Kingdom to build upon.

In practice: how is fieldwork introduced in Key Stage 1?

'In Year 1 we learn about simple maps and start by looking at aerial views of the school grounds. We teach pupils to use the four points of a compass. We explore the school grounds with our compasses so pupils can begin to develop a sense of direction and link what they saw on the aerial views to what they can experience first-hand. This builds on pupils' experiences in EYFS where they explored the school grounds searching for different leaves. We sketch maps of the school grounds and model how to use locational and directional language when describing locations on our sketch maps. Although we haven't left the school grounds at this point, pupils are developing the fieldwork skills they need for Key Stage 2.

Following this, in Year 2 pupils go on a walk around the local area. First, we look at maps and plan our route, identifying key human and physical features that pupils will see on that walk. We model using locational and directional language when *discussing our routes, building on learning from Year 1. We use compasses again; pupils are usually quite confident using them at this stage. Our walk gives pupils many opportunities to see their local area first hand and to use the geographical language we have modelled. When we are back at school, pupils sketch simple maps of the local area and we show them how to include a key. You can see the progress in map skills from Year 1 to Year 2 and pupils really enjoy drawing their maps.'*

In this example, fieldwork has been clearly and purposefully planned. Teachers have thought about how pupils will make progress in this area of geography. Pupils have the opportunity to build on their learning across the key stage as they become proficient at using a compass, draw maps and use geographical language.

Key Stage 2

The geography curriculum in Key Stage 2 will build on pupils' learning from Key Stage 1. To meet National Curriculum in England requirements pupils will extend their knowledge of the UK and will learn about Europe, North and South America. They will continue to develop their fieldwork skills progressing to using eight points of a compass, grid references and more data-based methods to measure and record the geography of the local area. As leaders, we must understand how our Key Stage 2 curriculum builds on from Key Stage 1 and how pupils learn and remember more over time.

In practice: how do pupils in Key Stage 2 build on their knowledge of the UK?

'In Key Stage 1, pupils learned about the countries and capital cities of the UK. They learned about some of the human and physical features of the UK, including the Welsh valleys and Scottish lochs.

In lower Key Stage 2 pupils build on this knowledge and study some of the regions of the UK, including the south east where they look at land use including the draining of the Fens and farming in East Anglia, and the south west where they look at features of the coastline and tourism. This helps pupils to see how some of these aspects have changed over time.

In upper Key Stage 2, pupils study some geographical issues in the context of the UK, including flooding, air pollution and waste management. They rely on their locational knowledge of the UK when studying these issues as they work with maps, graphs and data to understand the issues and the challenges they present. If pupils hadn't already mastered locational knowledge of the UK, studying these issues may cause cognitive overload, or pupils may just have a surface level understanding. Their knowledge of the UK, built over time by the carefully sequenced curriculum, supports their understanding and helps them to understand more complex geographical issues.'

In this example, it is possible to see how knowledge of the UK is carefully structured within the curriculum to help pupils learn more about the UK as they journey through the curriculum. Their locational knowledge forms the foundation for understanding complex geographical issues such as flooding in upper Key Stage 2. Studying an issue such as flooding in the UK without secure locational knowledge would be challenging for pupils, as they would not understand where places were in relation to one another and how locations are connected. This illustrates the importance of sequencing knowledge to ensure pupils have secure frameworks of understanding to build upon as they work through the curriculum.

In practice: how does pupils' place knowledge develop in Key Stage 2?

'In Key Stage 1, pupils began to understand geographical similarities and differences when they studied our local area and compared it with San Francisco. They have continued to build their place knowledge when studying the human and physical features of regions of the UK in lower Key Stage 2, including East Anglia and the Dorset coastline.

In lower Key Stage 2, pupils study Poland and focus on Warsaw. We chose to study Poland as we have a number of Polish families in our school community; parents have come in to share photographs and memories of their childhood in Poland to enhance our pupils' understanding. We look at geographical similarities and differences between Warsaw and Birmingham.

Following this, in upper Key Stage 2 we study Anchorage, Alaska as a region within North America. We chose Anchorage as it provides great contrast for our pupils to learn about a coastal city after studying both Birmingham and Warsaw. Pupils learned about San Francisco in Key Stage 1, so knowledge of shipping, trade and ports can be applied to this new context. We also wanted pupils to learn about the location of Anchorage and its proximity to Asia and particularly Russia, as we know pupils can have a misconception that the continent of North America is far from Asia as the two are often represented on either ends of a map of the world.'

In this example thought has been given to the places that fit the requirements of the National Curriculum in England, but also to places that are meaningful for the pupils in school. Including a study on Poland and Warsaw allows this school to make links to their pupils' experience of the world and also allows families to contribute to the curriculum. Leaders in this school have also considered pupils' spatial misconceptions and how to rectify these by highlighting the proximity of Russia and North America.

As subject leaders we can probe our curriculum and find out:

- which places pupils learn about
- what they learn about those places
- how that knowledge provides a foundation for future learning.

Case study: implementing a new scheme of work

Ciaran is a geography subject lead at a two-form entry school in Peterborough.

His school has followed a topic approach with half termly topics covering various foundation subjects for the past six years.

Pupil voice has revealed that pupils cannot identify things they have learned that relate to geography. They cannot describe the subject of geography beyond 'learning about countries'. Their place knowledge is limited. Ciaran finds it hard to identify how pupils make progress in geography within the current curriculum.

Ciaran shares his concerns with his key stage leader and talks to some of his colleagues. They agree that there is no clear progression within the topic approach and that pupils wouldn't necessarily know they are learning geography as the lessons are referred to as 'topic'.

The senior leaders in the school meet to discuss curriculum design. They identify where geography features in the different topics within the school curriculum. Through doing this, Ciaran recognises that currently, the National Curriculum in England is not being covered in its entirety.

In collaboration with his Senior Leadership Team (SLT), Ciaran suggests ways in which the geography content within the current topics could be expanded to cover the National Curriculum in England. For example, when studying 'The Romans', teachers will use atlases to teach locational knowledge of Europe so pupils can understand where the Roman Empire spread.

He plans a staff meeting geography session for teachers where they can look at their topics and identify where there are further opportunities for geography to be taught. He shares the National Curriculum in England with staff so each key stage can check they are teaching the required content and address any gaps.

In the future, Ciaran would like to hold a session that looks at how local geography is woven through the topic structure. In doing so, he will identify places and geographical features that are locally relevant.

Chapter summary

- This chapter has explored how you can reflect on the design of our geography curriculum in order to understand how content is chosen, structured and sequenced.

- We have highlighted the importance of understanding the thinking behind curriculum design, both for purchased schemes and for curriculum design and development within school.

- We have explored curriculum content choices – the places, geographical features and processes pupils will learn about.

- We have explored why it is important we know the specific content of your geography curriculum.

- We have considered curriculum structure and how a curriculum is organised.

- We have reflected on curriculum sequencing; the order in which geography content is placed to support learning over time.

Questions for reflection

- Which places do our pupils learn about within our curriculum and why?
- How is our geography curriculum structured?
- How is our geography curriculum sequenced from EYFS to Key Stage 2?

Example PD session: understanding geography curriculum design

Here is an example of what a PD session on understanding geography curriculum design could look like.

TIMING SUGGESTION	SESSION GUIDANCE
10 mins	Share the whole school geography curriculum map. Explore how knowledge and understanding builds over time by following one or more of these threads through the curriculum: • Local geography • UK geography • World geography • Fieldwork Consider the question: *How has our school geography curriculum been designed?*
5 mins	Discuss specific geography content relevant to the local area and highlight the importance of embedding local knowledge in the curriculum. Consider the question: *Which places in our local area are important for our pupils to know?*
15 mins	Ask teachers to choose a geography unit they teach and then explain how it fits in the sequence of the curriculum. How does it build on previous learning and create a foundation for future learning? Use this to reveal the importance of the content taught in each unit.
20 mins	Give teachers time to explore the links between their units within their own year groups and other units across the curriculum. Ask teachers to create some questions that could be used in each unit to check on prior learning from within that year group, within the key stage or beyond. This will help teachers to learn from the curriculum design and use their knowledge to capitalise on pupils' prior learning. Provide an opportunity for peer feedback.

Explore further

- The Geographical Association's 'Planning a high quality primary geography curriculum'
- Royal Geographical Society's 'Starting to plan primary geography'
- The TED talk 'The danger of a single story' (2009) by Chimamanda Adiche
- *Working with the Revised Early Years Foundation Stage: Principles into Practice* (2020 by Julian Grenier

6 Geography for all: scaffolding for success

In this chapter, we will explore ways in which we can probe our geography curriculum and the provision within our classrooms to ensure we are scaffolding for success for all pupils.

Within the primary classroom it is highly likely there will be pupils with special educational needs and those who have additional needs that have not yet been officially recognised. Alongside these pupils there may be others with needs caused by other factors, such as a school move or other disruption in their lives. Therefore, we must carefully consider how we adapt our geography curriculum offer to ensure it is accessible for the wide range of needs our pupils may have. As subject leaders we must also understand how we can support our colleagues to deliver an inclusive geography curriculum that provides challenge for all pupils, regardless of their starting point.

In this chapter we will cover:

- scaffolding in the geography classroom
- differentiation and adaptation
- adaptations for pupils who are yet to secure adequate prior knowledge
- scaffolding ideas for pupils with speech and language challenges
- scaffolding ideas for pupils who struggle with writing
- scaffolding ideas to support pupils with vision or hearing impairments.

Scaffolding in the geography classroom

Within your classrooms, all pupils will be working towards a goal within a geography lesson, but some may need particular support, tailored to their needs, to achieve this goal. For example, a pupil who is learning English as an additional language may benefit from a word bank with images to support them to access vocabulary; a pupil who struggles to organise their ideas when writing may need a structured plan to work from when writing independently. Scaffolding means considering individual pupils' needs and creating tools, or scaffolds, to help them reach the shared goal alongside their peers. Scaffolds should be temporary and adaptable; once a pupil is confident and capable a scaffold can be removed.

Some pupils will need approaches to teaching and learning in geography to be adapted based on their specific SEND. As described by the National Association of Special Educational Needs (NASEN) 'labels in themselves do not offer us a complete picture of the pupil and in fact, an individual's needs may be different to the general characteristics of their labelled 'condition' (NASEN, nd). Therefore, we cannot suggest a particular scaffold will be helpful for all pupils with a given diagnosis. We must consider how we adapt and scaffold for pupils' needs on a case-by-case basis in school.

As geography leaders we can have oversight of the range of scaffolds available to teachers to support teaching and learning in geography. It is our responsibility to consider ways in which our subject is inclusive and to take further steps to ensure we scaffold for the success of every pupil.

Differentiation and adaptation

Differentiation refers to the process of providing differing support towards an end goal. Sometimes this is referred to as making adaptations.

In the past, the term 'differentiation' has on occasion been misinterpreted, with some teachers creating different tasks within a lesson for groups of pupils, resulting in varying levels of required effort and different outcomes. The problem with this approach is that pupils can be assigned a task, based on their perceived 'ability' which is often inaccurate and places a ceiling on what they can achieve. Pupils are also often aware that they have been allocated an 'easier' task compared to others which impacts on self-esteem and self-belief.

Recently, there has been a move to reclaim the word 'differentiation' to describe the different scaffolds a teacher may put in place to support pupils to work towards a shared goal. In this context, differentiation is about focussing on the different ways in which pupils can be supported to access a task and achieve success.

In the National Curriculum in England, it states, 'A wide range of pupils have special educational needs, many of whom also have disabilities. Lessons should be planned to ensure that there are no barriers to every pupil achieving' (DfE, 2013). In the SEND code of practice, it states, 'High quality teaching that is differentiated and personalised will meet the individual needs of the majority of children and young people' (DfE and DoH, 2014). It goes on to explain that some pupils will need additional or different provision and this is special educational provision.

As a geography leader, it is helpful to consider how to remove barriers to success for pupils with additional or special needs. Adaptations within lessons, small changes that are targeted to specific needs, allow teachers to maintain the integrity of the lesson, avoid assigning 'different' tasks, and can be carefully planned to scaffold around the task that all pupils are engaged in.

Adaptations for pupils who are yet to secure adequate prior knowledge

Prior knowledge is knowledge we already have established; it is the 'things we know'. For our pupils, prior knowledge might come from lessons we have taught, lessons from previous years, books or independent learning, experiences outside of school or many other sources. What we know directly impacts what we learn. John Hattie's research supports this; he found, in fact, prior knowledge has a bigger impact on learning than differences in IQ' (Hattie et al., 2013).

Paul Kirshner and Carl Hendrick explain the role of prior knowledge: 'In order to create rich and coherent knowledge schemes, students must actively insert now information into existing knowledge structures' (Kirschner et al., 2020, p.59) As a subject leader, it is important to know at each stage of the curriculum what pupils have already studied and therefore what they should know, so you can check on this.

Graham Nuthall's classroom-based research over forty years revealed that on average pupils know approximately 50 percent of what a teacher plans on teaching. However, that 50 percent is not evenly distributed; different pupils know different amounts of different things (Nuthall, 2007). This reveals the complexities of teaching: pupils know many different things and there are, on average, 30 pupils sat in front of each teacher, so that is a lot of variation within one class. This might sound familiar to you!

Within your classrooms there may well be pupils who have not yet secured adequate prior knowledge in geography. Some pupils arrive mid-year and have not learned previously taught content at their previous school or when arriving from overseas. Some pupils may have not secured knowledge and understanding for other reasons.

As outlined above, prior knowledge is a hugely important consideration, and its importance has implications for our primary geography lessons. Although we cannot ever really know for sure exactly what every pupil in our class knows at any given time, the curriculum should specify the content they have previously studied. This enables us to check specific knowledge before introducing new content. An example of this would be a pupil trying to learn about earthquakes before understanding that the ground we walk on sits on large tectonic plates. You could simply explain that the ground shakes during an earthquake, but for any meaningful understanding of this to be present, a pupil would need to know about tectonic plates and how they behave to enable them to understand how and why earthquakes occur at plate boundaries.

We have established the importance of checking prior knowledge and if necessary, making adaptations in the moment. Whilst knowing the pupils we teach is one important way to support their learning, checking for prior knowledge and not making assumptions about their prior learning is also important. Building in an opportunity to check prior learning into every geography lesson will help teachers to understand which pupils may need extra support or adaptations. It also provides an opportunity for all pupils to reconnect to their prior learning and understand where the new learning will build on what they already know.

As a subject leader, we can look for how teachers check prior knowledge if we have the opportunity to observe colleagues teaching.

In practice: example of adapting for prior knowledge

- Pupils are going to be learning about the landscape of the east of England.
- The teacher asks pupils to identify the countries of the UK and locate some key cities using cardinal directions (North, South, East and West) to describe their locations. (For example England is located to the south of Scotland. London is the capital city and is located in the south of England.)

- The teacher notices a pupil who cannot identify the countries of the UK, so they open an atlas and show the pupil a map of the UK whilst other pupils are identifying the countries from memory. The teacher identifies countries, orally rehearsing their names briefly, and provides a printed compass with the directions labelled.
- The teacher shows pupils the same pictures of the mountainous landscape in Scotland that were studied in a previous unit. This helps all pupils to remember key features of the landscape in some of the northern regions of the UK.
- The teacher then introduces new learning, confident that all pupils are ready to learn about the east of England.
- Towards the end of the lesson, the teacher returns to the pupil and asks them if they can find England and then the east of England on a map of the UK in their atlas. The pupil can do this. The teacher makes a note to check this knowledge again at an opportune moment, using the map of the UK on the working wall.

Action points

As a subject leader, these are some key questions to ask:

- What have pupils already learned in geography?
- How can I find out if they know and remember it?
- How do I help pupils who don't have this prior knowledge?

Scaffolding ideas for pupils with speech and language challenges

An important aspect of geography is communication. Geographers find out about the world and then share what they have found through contributing to reports, documentaries, news articles, research projects and more. There are many elements of speech and language within geography that we can offer support with which will benefit all pupils but particularly those with additional needs. Some examples are outlined in the table below.

In practice: questions to consider for pupils with speech and language challenges

Speech and language elements	Questions to consider:
Introduction of new vocabulary	Is a list of new vocabulary available to support staff before the lesson? How is new vocabulary taught to the whole class? (For example do pupils use actions? Are there supporting visuals?) How many words on average are pupils taught in a geography lesson? (Have we considered cognitive load?) Is the vocabulary put into a sentence and modelled by the teacher?
Opportunities to use and apply recently learned vocabulary	Are pupils expected to orally rehearse the new words? Do pupils have an opportunity to orally rehearse with a partner? Will pupils be expected to write the new vocabulary later in the lesson? Where can pupils access the new vocabulary during the lesson? (For example on a word bank, knowledge organiser or working wall.)
Modelling of subject-specific vocabulary in different contexts	Do we offer multiple examples when introducing subject-specific vocabulary? Example: **Migration** means to move from one place to another. Animal **migration** is often linked to seasonal changes; some animals seek warmer weather for parts of the year. Human **migration** is often based on a search for work, or a desire for a different place to live. Sometimes migration occurs as a result of conflict within a region, or environmental disaster such as drought.
Process-based language, for example X occurs which causes Y and this has impact on Z Example: A high level of rainfall in a short period of time can cause flooding, which has impact on people living and working in the surrounding areas.	When pupils are learning about geographical processes, do we model the grammar structures we want them to be using? When writing about processes, can we provide a visual support to help pupils organise their thoughts, language and then writing? (For example pictures representing each stage of a process that pupils order.)

Speech and language elements	Questions to consider:
Directional and positional language	Do we model using directional and positional language? Examples: France is located **to the south** of the UK **Between** the lake and the road there is a forest. If you travel **to the north**, **past** the bridge, you will find the park. It is **close to** the church.
Analytical language	Can we provide models, oral rehearsal and then sentence stems for pupils who need support with language? Examples: **The data shows… this suggests that… the evidence we found highlights…**

Within a geography lesson, key vocabulary will sometimes include new words for pupils to learn, at other times the words will have been taught before and pupils will be applying them in new contexts.

When teaching pupils with specific speech and language needs, it is vital to check which methods of instruction and what modes of scaffolding have been recommended for individuals. For example, a pupil may benefit from visual support and therefore when introducing new words the teacher may use a picture and an action alongside each new word. Some pupils may use digital programmes that play audio files of new words being spoken. We will explore the teaching of vocabulary in geography in Chapter 10. Many of the suggestions will support all pupils, particularly those with additional speech and language needs.

Action points

It may be helpful for you to consider these following action points as you lead geography within your school:

- Meet with senior leaders including the SENDCo in your school to discuss how school-wide initiatives for supporting speech and language development can be implemented in geography lessons.

- Ensure key vocabulary is identified for each geography lesson or unit of work. Consider how this vocabulary is taught and what opportunities pupils have to orally rehearse and apply the vocabulary in different contexts.

- Identify when pupils would be expected to use process-based language to explain geographical processes or findings from fieldwork.
- Look at the English curriculum and identify where specific grammar is taught that would be useful to apply in a geography context.

Scaffolding ideas for pupils who struggle with writing

Geographers write to record their research and to communicate it to a wide variety of audiences, including policy makers, businesses, engineers, local governments and more. Geographers must be able to communicate effectively through writing as they need to tell the story of their work and why it is important for the world.

For pupils who find writing challenging, there are a number of strategies we can use in geography to support them to succeed. Some examples are outlined below.

In practice: ideas for pupils who struggle with writing

Oral rehearsal before writing	This strategy is helpful for all pupils but particularly for those who find writing challenging. Using teacher modelling then talk partners allows pupils to hear an example first, then try out the new word or specific sentence structure orally before writing. Example: 'A valley has sloping sides'. My turn: 'valley'; your turn (together) 'valley'. Show me a valley shape using your arms (pupils make a 'v' shape with their arms). Good. 'A valley has sloping sides'.
Note-taking	In KS2, pupils may benefit from using a whiteboard to take notes first. This needs to be explicitly taught first, to ensure pupils are able to identify the key information to note. They can then use their notes as a scaffold for their writing, possibly reducing the apprehension that some pupils feel when facing a blank page. Example: When preparing to write a description of the landscape in the Yorkshire Dales, a pupil could write some key notes in bullet point form including the location, shape of the land and physical features, such as moors, rivers.

Picture prompts for sequencing	If you are asking pupils to write about several different things in a particular order, consider providing picture prompts for pupils who may muddle the sequence of their writing. Example: When writing about the journey of a river from the source to the mouth, pupils may find picture prompts help them with the order of the features such as source, stream, river, waterfalls, rapids, meanders, floodplain and estuary.
Structure strips	A structure strip can be an effective scaffold for all pupils, particularly those who struggle with writing stamina. Provide paragraph headings and some key geographical words or content for each paragraph on a bookmark-sized piece of paper that pupils can place alongside their exercise books when writing. They can tick off each paragraph as they write it. This can help with organising longer pieces of writing.
Word banks	A word bank is helpful for pupils who need support with spelling key geographical words. A knowledge organiser could also be used as a resource for checking key words.
Sentence stems	Sentence stems provide the first part of a sentence, which pupils use to start their writing and then they complete the sentence with their own thoughts. They help pupils who struggle to get started with writing. Example: The population of Rio de Janiero is growing because… Madagascar experiences food insecurity due to… Irrigation of the Mississippi River has caused…
Scribing	If a pupil really struggles to write, you or another member of staff could scribe for them. This would provide a record of their geography knowledge, showing what they can tell you and perhaps revealing more understanding than they can write.

Action points

- What are children expected to write within the geography curriculum?
- How do we scaffold and support children's writing in geography?
- Do we offer alternative ways for children to show what they know if they are unable to complete a written task?

Scaffolding ideas to support pupils with vision or hearing impairments

Visual impairments

Geography, like many other primary subjects, requires the use of many different visual resources, such as maps, images, diagrams and charts. When selecting visual resources, it is important to consider the following ideas.

In practice: ideas to support pupils with visual impairments

Classroom seating	Consider whether all pupils, no matter where they are sat in the room, will be able to see resources, particularly if they are showing information on a board.
Large print	Pupils with a recognised vision impairment may benefit from using a large print atlas in geography lessons. It is also important to consider other printed resources provided in geography lessons, such as maps, graphs and data.
Colour contrast	Dunn and Darlington (2016) recommend that diagrams have clear black lines outlining the features of interest and that they use contrasting colours to aid visual accessibility. If teachers are using diagrams found on the internet, these may need to be adapted to be accessible for a pupil with visual impairment. (A resource for further reading on this is included at the end of the chapter.)
Central resource bank	As a geography leader, it could be helpful to set up a central resource of saved diagrams that teachers can use that are visually accessible. This bank could be added to as teachers find resources when planning their lessons.
Supporting adults	If a pupil with visual impairment has an adult supporting them in class, as a leader of geography you can ensure the curriculum content is shared in advance, so the supporting adult can prepare for the lessons by adapting and scaffolding for the individual's needs.

Action points

As a subject leader, these are some key questions to consider:

- Are videos used as a resource within our geography curriculum? Are these accessible? Do they have auditory support if pupils are unable to access them visually?
- Are printed resources (for example maps, data, word banks) accessible?
- How are images used within your geography curriculum? Are images largely shown on an interactive whiteboard? How can these be made accessible?

Hearing impairments

Some pupils within our schools may have hearing impairment. This may have been recognised and addressed by specialists or could be undiagnosed.

As subject leaders we can be mindful of how our geography lessons and classroom environments could be adapted to ensure they are inclusive for all pupils. For pupils with a supporting adult, such as a communication support worker or learning support assistant, ensure the adult has access to the geography curriculum in advance. This will enable the adult to identify key language that they may need to teach pupils to sign (if using British Sign Language or an equivalent). Teachers could share key vocabulary for specific lessons in advance, allowing the adult adequate preparation time.

Action points

As a subject leader, these are some key questions to consider:

- Can a hearing impaired pupil always see the teacher's face when they are talking? Are teachers using clear and uncluttered language when teaching and modelling?
- If using videos as part of a geography lesson, can the supporting adult see the content in advance so they can sign or support the pupil in another way with the auditory element of the video?
- Are there key words that the teacher could learn to sign?
- Are talk partners used within the geography lesson? If so, how can we support pupils with auditory impairments and how can their peers adapt to ensure this teaching and learning tool is inclusive? (For example having a hand signal to show a partner is going to talk, reducing background noise where possible, encouraging partners to repeat what they have said…)

Claire is a geography leader in a three form entry primary school in Kent.

She recently attended whole-school training on inclusion in primary schools. Although this training was not specific to geography, Claire wants to consider how some of the suggested strategies might support children with additional needs in their geography lessons.

As part of her leadership role, Claire observes two geography lessons, one in each key stage. She also asks colleagues to share children's books with her, including those with SEND.

Claire notices that during lesson time, some children were not focussed on the map the teacher was displaying on the board. Some children couldn't remember some key features of the map once the teacher had moved to the next slide on the board. In the books, Claire notices that some children with additional needs were not completing the independent tasks.

Claire meets with the special educational needs co-ordinator for a discussion about what she noticed in her observations and the conclusions she drew from looking at books.

Together, Claire and the SENDCo consider strategies for supporting during map work and during the independent tasks children are set to complete. These include using physical maps and atlases as much as possible, so children have these in front of them for the whole lesson. Adults working with children with SEND will be encouraged to print and use paper maps if an atlas is not relevant for that particular lesson. Claire plans to run a staff meeting on scaffolding tasks in geography to ensure all children can be successful. She will share strategies such as using sentence stems, word banks and picture prompts with staff. She will also explore ways in which children can show what they know in geography in addition to writing.

Claire plans some future observations to look specifically at children with SEND and their experience in their geography lessons.

Chapter summary

In this chapter we have explored the following:

- The importance of providing scaffolds for all children to succeed
- How we can support children with gaps in their prior learning
- How children with speech and language challenges can be supported
- Ideas for supporting children who struggle to write
- How we can adapt resources to support children with visual impairments

Questions for reflection

- How are children with SEND included in our geography lessons?
- What scaffolds and supports do we provide for children in geography?
- What specific SEND needs are there in my school and how can I ensure geography lessons are accessible?

Example PD session: scaffolding for success in geography

Here is an example of what a PD session on scaffolding for success in geography could look like.

TIMING SUGGESTION	SESSION GUIDANCE
10 mins	Read the EEF blog 'Moving from 'differentiation' to 'adaptive teaching'' (Eaton, 2022).
5 mins	Discuss how and why this might be relevant to geography teaching, referring to the specific topics/units of work within specific year groups.

TIMING SUGGESTION	SESSION GUIDANCE
15 mins	Create a list of different ways geography lessons could be adapted for pupils with specific needs (for example using word banks, printed maps, working walls, pre-teaching vocabulary, sentence stems) and ask teachers to discuss which is most appropriate for the needs within their own class. Ask SENDCo to input any relevant ideas/techniques.
20 mins	Give teachers the opportunity to create some resources required for adaptations for their forthcoming geography lessons/unit. They plan/script how they will introduce these to specific pupils. Provide opportunity for peer feedback.

Explore further

- The EEF's 'Communication and language: approaches and practices to support communication and language development in the early years' (2024c)

- The National Deaf Children's Society's 'Deaf-friendly teaching: for primary school staff' (2020)

- Training and Development Agency's 'Including pupils with SEN and/or disabilities in primary geography' (2009)

- Macular Society's 'General tips for teaching vision impaired students' (2025)

More advice on good practice in primary schools to support children with vision impairments can be found here: https://www.birmingham.ac.uk/research/cent res-institutes/vision-impairment-centre-for-teaching-and-research/resources/ best-practice-in-supporting-students-with-vision-impairment.

7 Map work

This chapter will explore how we can use maps effectively in our classrooms. Maps are a wonderful resource for pupils of all ages; they encourage visual and spatial thinking whilst developing knowledge of the world around us. In a modern classroom, with the internet at our fingertips, we can show pupils any corner of the earth in moments. With careful thought and planning, we can supplement the use of physical maps, atlases and globes with digital maps, enriching our teaching and supporting pupils' learning.

This chapter will explore:

- introducing map work (including types of map)
- map work in the classroom (using atlases, globes, OS maps and digital mapping)
- progression in map work.

Introducing map work

A map is a drawing of the surface of the earth and its features. Maps are drawn from an aerial perspective; they show us what an area would look like from above. Maps do not depict what features of an area look like in detail; they use symbols or representations to communicate what is located in a particular area. The art of map making is called cartography.

Humans have created maps for thousands of years to record, explain and navigate the world around them. Some of the oldest surviving maps include etchings on a mammoth tusk found in the Czech Republic and dating back to 25,000 BC (National Geographic Society, 2025), and an Aboriginal Australian cylcon (conical shaped stone with etchings) thought to show the Darling River and estimated to be approximately 20,000 years old (The Schoyen Collection). Of course, we cannot be sure that these artefacts were maps, but evidence indicates humans were recording their understanding of geographical areas in prehistoric times. In later periods, maps were created by the Ancient Greeks,

Babylonians, and Egyptians as people farmed land, traded and as territory became a source of power. Therefore, when using maps with pupils, we are engaging in an activity that is thousands of years old.

In modern times, we have maps of every corner of the earth accessible to us at the touch of a button. We carry the world in our pockets and use technology to plan routes and navigate with ease. With this in mind, we could ask why should we teach map work to primary pupils?

Sketch mapping

Maps are an organisational and informational tool that help young pupils to understand their immediate area and beyond. Research has shown that very young children create cognitive maps that are 'dependent on the recall and reconstruction of children's experience of place' (Boardman, 1989). These mental maps can be translated onto paper when pupils are asked to draw their home or school.

This type of map work, where mental maps are translated onto paper is known as sketch mapping. In primary schools, pupils might be asked to draw a sketch map of their journey to school, or a character's journey through a familiar story setting. These tasks require pupils to identify what is located in a particular area, which supports their understanding of spatial relationships, or spatial sense, such as the distance between locations, what is located in between two different places, what is near to and far from particular features on a map. These early map skills help young pupils to gain a sense of where they are and what is around them.

Types of map

Over time, developing spatial sense helps pupils to understand not only place, but space. This helps them to understand where they are and where other things happening in the world are, what is nearby and what is far away. In a world of accessible media this helps pupils to place things around the world. Although technology has made maps far more accessible for pupils now, it is vital that they have conceptual understanding of what maps represent so they can use them successfully to interact with and navigate the world around them.

In practice: types of maps that could be used in primary geography

Map type	Definition	Uses	Considerations
Aerial photographs	A photograph taken from the air, above the land.	Useful in EYFS and KS1 to support understanding of spatial relationships. Pupils can see where specific features are in relation to one another. As this type of map is a picture, it doesn't require pupils to understand abstract symbols, letters or numbers.	Consider having printed versions of aerial photographs on tables in the classroom, rather than showing only temporarily on an interactive whiteboard. This helps pupils to pinpoint locations with their fingers and enables them to refer back to them throughout the lesson.
Sketch maps	A roughly drawn map, drawn from observation or memory. Sketch maps are not detailed and do not have a high degree of accuracy.	Teachers can model how to draw a sketch map whilst explaining the thought process behind each feature of the map as they draw. Sketch maps don't need to be accurate or drawn to scale.	Some pupils may want to draw detailed pictures on their sketch maps and will spend too much time on details. Encourage them to 'sketch' and think more about the placement of features on their maps.
OS maps	Ordnance Survey is the national mapping agency of Great Britain. OS maps are used for many different purposes, including local or regional travel, outdoor activities such as hiking, and for planning purposes.	Suitable for use in KS1 and KS2, these maps support delivery of the National Curriculum objectives. OS maps can be used to study the local area, to plan routes, to identify physical and human features of a location, to study scale, and much more.	Using OS maps over time across year groups helps pupils to learn and remember more as they make progress. OS maps contain a wealth of information and can be used in many different contexts.

Map work

Map type	Definition	Uses	Considerations
Relief maps	A relief map shows the height of land, or elevation, through shading. High and low areas of land can be identified using a key.	These are particularly useful in KS2 for pupils who are learning about different physical features and how land compares and contrasts in different regions. Example: look at a relief map of East Anglia. What do you notice about the land? Why are large portions of the land in East Anglia used for agriculture? Would this be possible in the Yorkshire Dales?	Support understanding by showing pupils a political map alongside a relief map, so they can see where settlements are located and their relationship with the shape of the land. For example, are there many towns in the mountains of Wales? Where are major settlements in Wales located and why?
Geographical information	Maps showing geographical data such as life expectancy, population, access to clean water, and rainfall.	In upper KS2 pupils can apply their knowledge from science and maths to engage with maps that show geographical information. They can apply their locational knowledge and find out which areas of the world are highly populated, or which areas do not have access to clean water. Interacting with these maps helps pupils see patterns and distribution across the world and also supports their understanding of how geographers use maps to communicate information.	Pupils will use knowledge of handling data from maths and science in geography. Ensuring they are confident with using percentages, numbers over 1000, keys and graphs will help to improve fluency when reading geographical information maps.

Map work in the classroom

It is helpful to consider when and why map work features within your geography curriculum from EYFS through to Key Stage 2:

- Do you leave the choice of maps down to chance or specify which types of maps pupils will engage with?
- Does your curriculum specify which types of maps pupils will encounter at a given point in the curriculum?
- Do pupils have the prior knowledge required for them to access the maps they will work with or is there a lot of additional information they may not understand?
- Which map skills will be explicitly taught and then practised within a given unit of work?

Atlases

Atlases are an incredibly useful resource in the primary classroom. It is helpful to have class sets of one type of atlas as this provides consistency and supports good classroom practice: pupils can follow clear instructions to find the correct page, rather than teachers scrambling to find a map of the UK on different pages in different atlases for thirty pupils.

In today's digital world it is cheaper and perhaps easier to find a map from a search engine and display it on an interactive whiteboard, however, this misses the opportunity for pupils to become confident using atlases.

When pupils skim through maps they have already studied, they are recalling prior learning. They then locate a given page, see the map in front of them and interpret that map with teacher guidance. The atlas can be open on pupils' tables as they work, allowing for further interaction, unlike a map shared on an interactive whiteboard.

An atlas contains a wealth of information that can be used to stretch and challenge those who need it, whilst also offering clear, visual support. An atlas is a treasure trove of interesting information that can be used outside of geography lessons, for example during independent reading time, offering more exposure to rich content and supporting long term learning.

Using atlases in EYFS

- First atlases and infant atlases are useful to use with EYFS as they are simplified, allowing pupils to explore and engage in an imaginative way.

- Atlases can be used as a conversation prompt, harnessing pupils' curiosity and offering opportunities to develop language.
- Young pupils can begin to develop an understanding of aerial views and spatial positioning (for example Australia is really far away from where we live in England).

Using atlases in Key Stage 1

- When locating maps of the world, pupils are becoming familiar with using contents pages to find the maps they are looking for.
- When locating maps of the UK, pupils search through an atlas and see lots of maps of places that are not the UK, which helps them gain stronger understanding.
- When identifying specific continents and countries, pupils are securing their knowledge of the shape of land, locational understanding, directional understanding and place names.

Using atlases in Key Stage 2

- When locating continents, countries and places, pupils use the contents page with confidence and also begin to use the index page as a tool for locating places.
- Pupils can engage with data in atlases, such as temperature and rainfall, population, farming, industry and climate.
- In many school atlases, pupils can look at relief and political maps side by side, layering information about physical and human geographical features. This helps them to make connections between landscape and how people interact with it.

Action points

As a subject leader, these are some key questions to consider:

- Do we have quality atlas provision in our school? (Check the dates of atlases in school, including in the library.)
- Do we use infant atlases in EYFS and Key Stage 1?

- Are the atlases used in the school consistent, supporting pupils' cognitive load as they become fluent when using them? (If provision is not consistent, investigate prices of atlases from school suppliers and discuss purchasing the atlases you need with SLT. Ideally have one type of atlas for the whole class to streamline their use.)
- Does every year group have access to class sets of atlases for their geography lessons?
- If year groups are sharing atlases, is geography timetabled to enable this?
- How do we make sure the class sets are all returned to the correct place and not absorbed into classrooms?
- Are there atlases available to pupils for independent reading time?

Globes

A globe is a three-dimensional representation of the world. Globes are often attached to a support which enables pupils to see that the earth is tilted on an axis and rotates at a slight angle as it orbits the sun. Globes help pupils to 'accurately understand the relative locations of places' (Robertson et al., 2019).

Using globes in EYFS

- In Montessori nursery education, based on the work of Maria Montessori (Association Montessori Internationale, 2023), pupils in the early years are first introduced to what is known as the sandpaper globe (Montessori Academy, 2017), before being introduced to a globe with each continent represented by a different colour. On a sandpaper globe, the land is all one sand colour, and the oceans are blue. This helps pupils to distinguish between land and water first, before progressing to recognising the different shape of the continents.
- A globe can be used to show pupils where places are around the world at opportune moments, such as when having conversations about places they have been, or where family members live. If pupils read books about animals in the arctic, a globe can be used to show them where the poles are, and they can discuss what it might be like to live in those places.

Using globes in Key Stage 1

- Building on their experiences in EYFS, pupils can begin to identify where we live on a globe.
- When studying different places, pupils can identify them on both a flat map and a globe to support their understanding and locational knowledge.

Using globes in Key Stage 2

- Building on their locational knowledge from Key Stage 1, pupils can use globes to become familiar with geographical tools such as lines of latitude, longitude, the equator and the hemispheres.
- Globes can support pupils' understanding of orbit and rotation, helping them to understand seasonal changes, night and day and climate.
- Pupils can study map projection and understand the challenges of representing a three-dimensional earth on a flat map.

Action points

As a subject leader, these are some key questions to consider:

- Does every classroom, including in EYFS, have a globe?
- Do the globes in school have more detail in upper Key Stage 2 than in EYFS?

OS maps

Ordnance Survey is the national mapping agency of Great Britain. The word 'ordnance' means military supplies, and the mapping agency has its origins from a military survey of the Scottish Highlands during the Jacobite rebellion in 1745 (Ordnance Survey, 2023). Knowing the shape of the land is important from a military perspective; knowledge of where your enemies are likely to invade and where your points of vantage are helps to form strategy. During the French Revolution, the British government were concerned that the conflict might reach England's southern coastline, so they ordered a survey of the area to create a detailed record of where the land might be vulnerable and where troops could be placed (Ordnance Survey, 2023). Now, OS maps are used for many different purposes, including local or regional travel, outdoor activities such as hiking, and for planning purposes.

For primary pupils, OS maps can help to unlock understanding of the local area and beyond. Over time, pupils can build knowledge and skills each time they interact with the maps. For example, pupils in Year 2 might learn some simple OS symbols relevant to their local area before tackling more challenging map reading in Key Stage 2, including calculating scale and using grid references. In upper Key Stage 2 pupils might look at features such as contour lines, building on their knowledge of relief maps and topography (the shape of land).

OS maps should be a consistent feature in the primary curriculum. Pupils should have many well-planned opportunities to interact with and learn from the maps, building understanding over time and helping them to make meaning.

You will need to ensure that pupils encounter OS maps each year with increasing understanding. Teachers may need support in developing their subject knowledge and being able to recognise and describe key symbols. You could provide a short 'teacher guide' setting out the key symbols and perhaps do short, fun quizzes for teachers on these at the beginning of staff meetings.

Using OS maps in EYFS

- OS maps are not specifically referenced in the EYFS curriculum, but areas of OS maps can be enlarged and used by pupils alongside other maps, atlases and globes.

- Young pupils will not fully understand the symbols on OS maps, but they can begin to explore the idea of symbols representing features on a map as they play. It may be that teachers prefer to use simple maps at this stage.

Using OS maps in Key Stage 1

- Pupils in Key Stage 1 can be introduced to OS maps of the local area, building on understanding they may have gained from looking at aerial views of the school and the surrounding area.

- Pupils can be taught some of the key symbols used on OS maps, for example roads, buildings, footpaths, places of worship.

- Pupils can begin to use directional and positional language to discuss the location of key places, including human and physical features of the local area.

Using OS maps in Key Stage 2

- Building on their prior knowledge from Key Stage 1, pupils in Key Stage 2 can explore OS maps further, understanding more features such as contours, grid references and scale.

- Pupils can use OS maps to explore places that are less familiar to them, moving on from knowledge of the local area and applying their maps skills to new areas.

Action points

As a subject leader, these are some key questions to consider:

- Is there a class set of OS maps in school?
- Are the maps stored centrally so teachers can easily access them?

Digital mapping

Digital maps are created by compiling information to create virtual maps. They are likely to be a very familiar format for pupils, one they have seen in the world around them many times. Like physical maps, digital maps show information about locations and both physical and human features of the land. Digital maps can be used to plan routes and calculate distances and travel times with ease.

The technological advancements we have seen in mapping has been described as the 'geospatial revolution' (Robertson et al., 2019). This revolution has implications for the way we teach pupils mapping and for the development of their spatial understanding. Physical printed maps still have an important role to play in the primary classroom, but we can enhance our teaching of map work to include digital mapping as pupils' understanding develops over time.

Digital OS maps are available through *Digimaps for Schools*, a subscription based digital mapping tool that provides digital modern day and historical maps alongside aerial images. Pupils can apply their knowledge of OS maps when using this digital tool for tasks such as plotting routes, identifying land use or looking at change over time in a particular location. Other digital mapping services are available online.

Through the use of digital maps, such as OS digimaps, we can show children maps of anywhere in the world with just a few clicks. Pupils can immediately access up-to-date maps, select criteria for the information they want to find out, zoom in from maps to see views of streets in countries all over the world and more. The scope of digital maps provides untold opportunities for our pupils to find out more about the world around them.

Geographic Information Systems (GIS)

Geographic Information Systems (GIS) are computer-based systems that collect, analyse and map geographic data relating to locations. GIS contain a map, layered data linked to locations and software that presents the information. GIS can be used in many ways to understand patterns, trends, relationships and geographical information. GIS can be used to study population change, rainfall, vegetation, forest fires, spread of a virus during a pandemic or pollution. Any issue that has a locational aspect could be studied using related data within GIS (Esri, 2021).

For primary pupils, particularly those in upper Key Stage 2, GIS can be used to find information when conducting a geographical enquiry. For example, pupils could use GIS to find out about population density in a particular region, the location and frequency of earthquakes around the world or migration patterns of animals. Using GIS, understanding how geographers work and how they use geographical information, will be built upon in Key Stage 3.

Action points

As a subject leader, these are some key questions to consider:

- Do GIS feature in our curriculum in upper Key Stage 2?
- What purpose do children use GIS for?
- What digital tools are available for teachers to teach GIS?

Progression in map work

When you are looking at your geography curriculum, it is helpful to identify how pupils progress in map work as they journey through the curriculum. As previously outlined, map work that pupils engage with in each year group should get increasingly more challenging and complex, building on prior knowledge. There should be time to practise and master the specific skills needed each time they work with maps.

You will need to support teachers to identify which map skills pupils will have ideally mastered and if there are any knowledge gaps that need to be filled before moving on. This helps all pupils, but particularly helps to close the gap for new starters to get them on track in geography as quickly as possible.

In practice: example of progression in map work

EYFS	Continuous provision activity: draw a map from memory for a familiar journey. On the table might be photos from the immediate and local area, aerial views of the school, simple maps of the local area, paper and pencils.

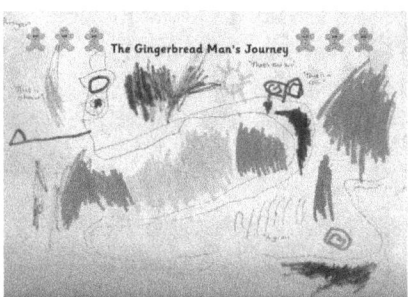

Figure 7.1a: The gingerbread man's journey

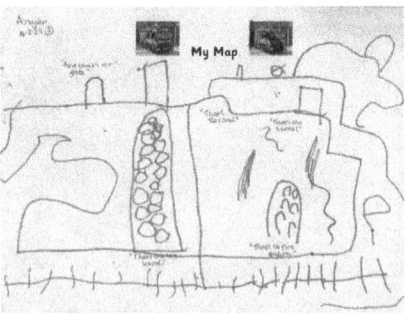

Figure 7.1b: A map drawn by a child in reception

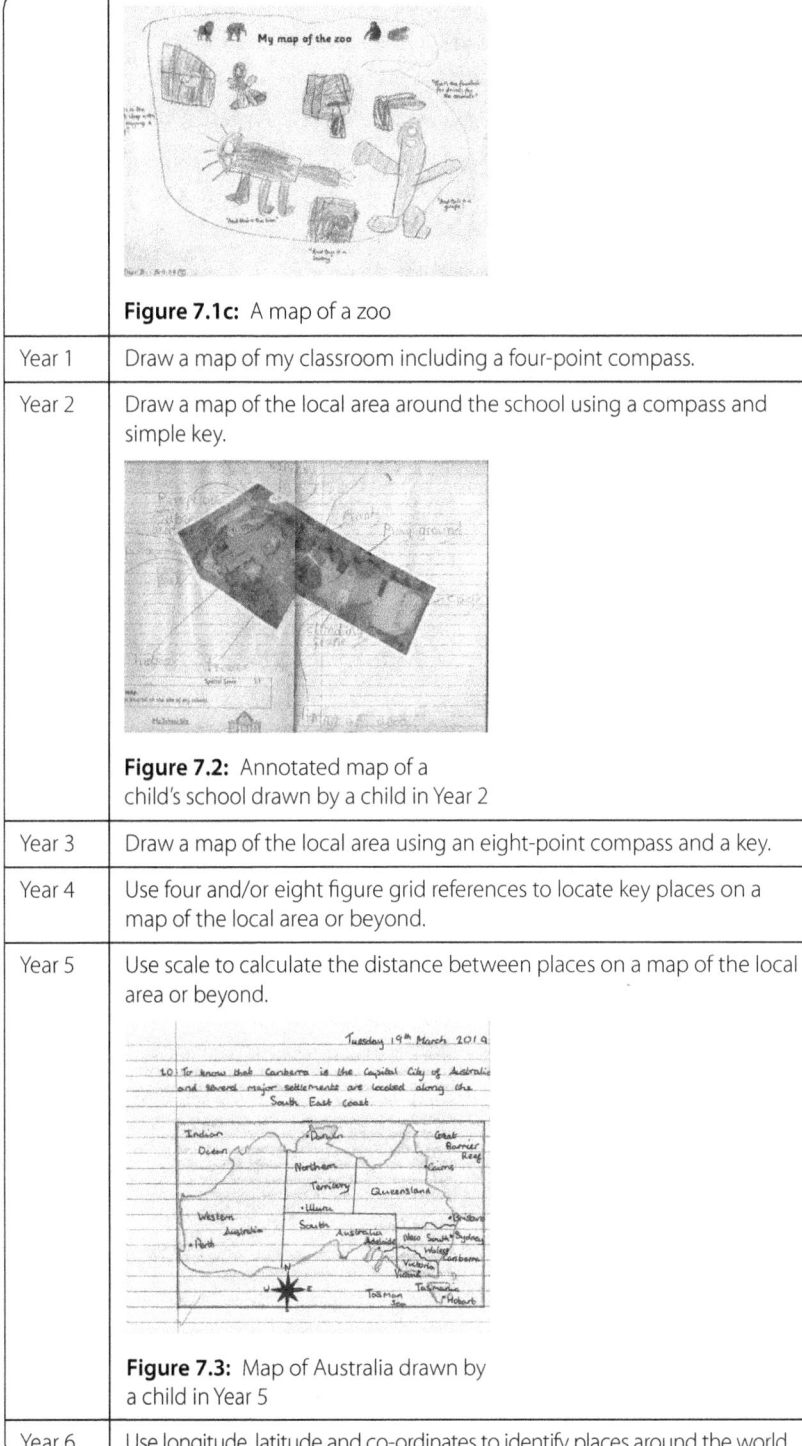

Figure 7.1c: A map of a zoo

Year 1	Draw a map of my classroom including a four-point compass.
Year 2	Draw a map of the local area around the school using a compass and simple key. **Figure 7.2:** Annotated map of a child's school drawn by a child in Year 2
Year 3	Draw a map of the local area using an eight-point compass and a key.
Year 4	Use four and/or eight figure grid references to locate key places on a map of the local area or beyond.
Year 5	Use scale to calculate the distance between places on a map of the local area or beyond. **Figure 7.3:** Map of Australia drawn by a child in Year 5
Year 6	Use longitude, latitude and co-ordinates to identify places around the world.

Writing in 1890, Sir Halford Mackinder argued that geography is not a collection of random information about places, but a 'trained capacity' for thought (Jones et al., 2018). This capacity for thought enables pupils, when looking at a map, to make meaning, to notice things, to understand beyond what they see in front of them.

We want primary pupils to understand the world around them, but also to make connections, notice patterns, ask questions, and perhaps suggest alternative futures. When thinking geographically, pupils will be drawing upon their understanding of place, space and the environment.

Peter Jackson explains that 'geography enables a unique way of seeing the world, of understanding complex problems and thinking about interconnections at a variety of scales' (Jackson, 2006). Map work has a crucial role to play in the process of thinking geographically and supporting pupils' growing understanding of the link between the visual representation of the world and the reality.

Action points

As a subject leader, these are some key questions to consider:

- Are the different map resources being used frequently?
- How do we know pupils are becoming more fluent with their atlas/globe/ map use as they move through the school? (For example, conduct some pupil voice to find out how familiar pupils are with maps/atlases.)

Chapter summary

- Map work can begin in EYFS with pupils engaging playfully with maps and becoming familiar with their immediate area.
- Map work can include (but isn't limited to): using aerial photographs, drawing sketch maps, engaging with OS maps, using relief maps, using digital mapping services and interpreting geographical information from maps using a key.
- When well planned, a geography curriculum will support pupils to make progress over time with map work.
- When following a curriculum planned as a progression model, pupils will learn and remember more with repeated opportunities to engage with map work, building knowledge and skills over time.

Questions for reflection

It may be helpful to consider the following when thinking about map work in your school:

- Which maps do children encounter in the curriculum?

- How are map skills taught in EYFS, Key Stage 1 and Key Stage 2?

- How do children make progress with their maps skills as they work through the curriculum?

- Do children work with maps and data in Key Stage 2? For example, do they work with population maps?

- How do children's encounters with maps help them to understand their local area and the wider world?

Example PD session: building progression in map work

Here is an example of what a PD session on building progression in map work could look like.

TIMING SUGGESTION	SESSION GUIDANCE
10 mins	Ask teachers to bring examples of map work to a staff meeting. Lay the examples out from EYFS through to Year 6. Ask teachers to look at the range of map work and discuss the different types of map work evidenced across the school.
5 mins	Highlight the sequence of the curriculum showing teachers how they contribute to progress over time as pupils build their knowledge and skills.
15 mins	As a team, answer this question: *How do pupils make progress in map work in our school?*
10 mins	Consider how to support pupils who have not secured map skills by looking back at the curriculum content that has come before and planning how to close the gaps.

Explore further

- 'Teaching map skills to inspire a sense of place and adventure' (2021) by Paula Owens
- Ordnance Survey map skills https://www.ordnancesurvey.co.uk/mapzone/map-skills
- Royal Geographical Society map skills https://www.rgs.org/schools/resources-for-schools/map-skills

8 Fieldwork

Fieldwork, as described by the Royal Geographical Society (nd), is 'the jewel in the crown of geography'. So, what does it look like in primary schools and what do we need to know as geography leaders?

Fieldwork can be defined as 'any curriculum component that involves leaving the classroom and engaging in teaching and learning activities through first-hand experiences of phenomena out-of-doors' (Lambert et al., 2014, p. 4). Fieldwork may involve transporting pupils to a particular location on a coach, bus or train to enjoy a full day of exploration, or it might be as simple as a walk around the school grounds, where there are many opportunities for geographical exploration.

When undertaking fieldwork, pupils will be learning and applying particular skills that feature in the discipline of geography, such as map reading, data collecting, measuring and more. These procedural skills support their disciplinary understanding as they reveal ways in which geographers work.

Fieldwork offers pupils opportunities to experience the world around them in ways that cannot be captured within the classroom with maps and pictures. This chapter will explore ways in which we can ensure fieldwork is planned well, undertaken skilfully and then reflected upon sufficiently to maximise the potential it holds to help our pupils connect to the world around them.

In this chapter we will cover the following points:

- the purpose of fieldwork in primary schools
- procedural knowledge
- sequencing fieldwork across the curriculum
- what effective fieldwork looks like
- how to risk assess fieldwork.

The purpose of fieldwork in primary schools

Fieldwork has been a feature of the school geography curriculum for many years (Cook, 2011). Over time, it has had dual purposes; firstly to educate pupils with geographical knowledge, and secondly to develop in them a sense of connection and responsibility as citizens. We want pupils to know and understand the world around them, but also to experience it, to feel it.

There are two areas of focus for fieldwork as leaders in primary schools:

- what knowledge pupils are learning
- what this work will make them think and feel.

Ultimately, we want pupils to enjoy fieldwork in primary school; to have positive experiences of geography and for fieldwork to enrich their learning and develop their interests. We are not working towards an examination or qualification in geography at primary level, therefore the scope of our work can focus on the experiences our pupils need in order to connect to the discipline of geography and to develop a love of geography that can continue into secondary school and beyond.

When reflecting on the purpose of fieldwork, it is important to consider why we want pupils to undertake it, what they will be doing and how they will reflect on the work they have done and the experiences they have had. Taking this approach shifts the focus from 'going on a trip', where practicalities become the focus, such as where to eat lunch (important but not the only consideration!), to a more methodical approach that helps pupils to see the ways in which geographers work, supporting disciplinary understanding.

Sharing the purpose of fieldwork with pupils is hugely important. Amongst the excitement of going off site and engaging in hands-on experiences, pupils need to understand why they are doing fieldwork; what questions are they trying to answer? What data are they collecting and why? What will they do with the information they find?

As geography lead, consider where fieldwork features in your curriculum and identify the specific elements of each episode of planned fieldwork. You may find that fieldwork is planned in terms of where pupils go, but it is unclear what exactly they will be doing. This can then be a focus for you to work with class teachers on the knowledge and skills pupils will gain. The table below is an example of what this could look like.

In practice: fieldwork in your curriculum

	Fieldwork example	Why do we want pupils to do this fieldwork? (reasoning and rationale)	What will pupils do when they are there? (procedural knowledge)	How will pupils reflect on their fieldwork? (analysing and communicating findings)
EYFS	Exploring school site	• To develop locational knowledge • To connect to the school site and familiarise themselves with it • To use directional and positional vocabulary	• Look at a site map of the school and locate their classroom • Plan a route together using the map to guide them • Apply knowledge of directional and positional language (for example: the hall is located to the left of the kitchens, past the office) • Take digital photos of places around the school site	• Look at photos from their journey around the school and talk about what they saw • Draw simple maps from memory

	Fieldwork example	Why do we want pupils to do this fieldwork? (reasoning and rationale)	What will pupils do when they are there? (procedural knowledge)	How will pupils reflect on their fieldwork? (analysing and communicating findings)
KS1	Exploring local area	• To build on their locational knowledge from EYFS • To build a connection to and identify key physical and human features within the local area • To use directional and positional vocabulary • To explore the four compass points • To understand how places are represented by symbols on maps	• Building on knowledge from EYFS, explore maps of the local area before their fieldwork • Identify key physical and human features on a map of the local area before their fieldwork • Plan a route to explore the local area using maps • Draw sketch maps whilst exploring the local area • Take photos and draw sketches of key physical and/or human features within the local area • Experience navigating around the local area using the four points of a compass and the related vocabulary • Notice particular issues relevant to their local area (for example: litter, parking, air pollution, empty shops, fly tipping)	• Sort the digital photos they took into human and physical features and describe them • Draw a map of the local area, using a key and symbols to represent key features • Write a report about the geography of their local area, including maps and pictures and expressing their opinions

	Fieldwork example	Why do we want pupils to do this fieldwork? (reasoning and rationale)	What will pupils do when they are there? (procedural knowledge)	How will pupils reflect on their fieldwork? (analysing and communicating findings)
KS2	Exploring contrasting area (rural/ urban) or specific geographical feature, such as a river	• To build on locational knowledge from KS1 • To apply geographical knowledge (including vocabulary) to explore an area that contrasts with the local area within which they live • To explore a specific issue relevant to the chosen area • To collect data • To use the eight points of a compass	• Gain first-hand experience of a contrasting area or specific geographical feature • Use and apply their map skills (for example, grid references, co-ordinates, symbols in a key) when planning and undertaking fieldwork • Collect data relating to a specific feature or issue in the area within which they are undertaking the fieldwork • Use the eight points of a compass to navigate, building on their knowledge and skills from KS1 • Discuss the features of the contrasting area or geographical feature using relevant geographical vocabulary • Take photos, sketch maps and draw diagrams, where relevant	• Analyse their data and draw graphs where relevant, to communicate their findings • Annotate maps and diagrams to show what they found in specific locations during their fieldwork • Write a report about the geography of the contrasting location or specific feature including maps, pictures and data, and make suggestions based on their experiences for improving an area/managing an issue

Procedural knowledge

When undertaking fieldwork, pupils are working in a way that develops procedural knowledge, often referred to as geographical skills. An example of this might be using a compass.

To use a compass effectively, pupils need to know:

- how to hold it flat in the palm of their hand
- how to identify the red end of the magnetic needle which points north and the white end which points south
- how to identify the direction they are travelling
- older pupils may then use the compass alongside a map to identify the direction of travel they must take to reach a destination.

Teaching this procedural knowledge explicitly in the classroom before pupils undertake fieldwork will equip them effectively, allowing them to use the fieldwork time as an opportunity to apply this knowledge.

The table below shows an example of how procedural knowledge has been planned in the curriculum. As subject lead, you may want to check that within your curriculum the knowledge pupils need is taught explicitly and that opportunities to apply the knowledge are present. If pupils are taught how to use four-figure grid references, but then never come back and apply them, they are likely to forget this procedural knowledge. It is helpful to consider how your curriculum supports long-term learning and to ensure pupils have multiple opportunities to apply their skills in different contexts.

Procedural knowledge could be mapped out onto a plan, as below, if useful, or it could be an action point for you to focus on as you work to develop your curriculum.

In practice: planning procedural knowledge

	National Curriculum requirements	Procedural knowledge/ geographical skills	When this will be taught	When will pupils practise and apply?
Using a compass (KS1)	Use simple compass directions (North, South, East and West) and locational and directional language (for example: near and far, left and right) to describe the location of features and routes on a map	• Hold the compass the correct way up, flat in the palm of your hand • Identify the red end of the magnetic needle which points north and the opposite (often white) end which points south • Turn the dial around until the 'N' aligns with the red end of the magnetic needle, then from this identify directions: north, south, east and west	Year 1 Autumn term Year 2 Autumn term	Year 1: end of Autumn term – fieldwork on school site Year 2: end of Autumn term – fieldwork in local area
Using grid references (KS2)	Use four- and six-figure grid references to build their knowledge of the UK and the wider world	• Identify the first letter or number in the grid reference, which tells you how far along the map you need to go (eastings) • Identify the second letter or number in the grid reference, which tells you how far up the map you need to go (northings) • For six-figure grid references, understand that the third and sixth numbers show a location within a square, and calculate in tenths across each easting and northing.	Year 4 Autumn term (four-figure) Year 5 Autumn term (six-figure)	Year 4: when studying the British Isles in the Spring term – four-figure grid references Year 5: use OS maps when studying local geography in the Spring term – six-figure grid references

	National Curriculum requirements	Procedural knowledge/ geographical skills	When this will be taught	When will pupils practise and apply?
Graphing data collected during fieldwork (KS2)	Use fieldwork to observe, measure and record the human and physical features in the local area using a range of methods, including sketch maps, plans and graphs and digital technologies	• Select which type of graph would be appropriate for the data collected (for example: line graphs show how data has changed over time, such as population change; bar charts show different categories, such as a traffic survey) • Understand how to draw the graph and insert the data • Be able to explain orally or with a written description, 'The graph shows that…'	Year 4 Spring term (line graphs) Year 5 Autumn term (bar chart and line graphs)	Year 4: look at population change in the local area and record the data on a line graph (Summer term) Year 5: select the most appropriate graph depending on the data they collect when studying local geography (Spring term)

Sequencing fieldwork across the curriculum

Nationally, the picture of fieldwork in the school curriculum is bleak. In both 2011 and 2023 Ofsted found that fieldwork was often not well planned and undertaken and that this was made even worse by the pandemic.

'Effective fieldwork supports pupils' motivation and enhances learning in geography…

Where fieldwork was properly conceived, adequately planned, well taught and followed up effectively, pupils were able to develop their knowledge and skills and the work added value to their classroom experiences. However, in just over half the schools visited, opportunities for fieldwork had decreased substantially in recent years.' Ofsted (2011, p. 41)

'Fieldwork was underdeveloped in almost all schools, as the curriculum did not consider how pupils would make progress in their ability to carry out fieldwork over time. Although COVID-19 had an impact on the number of field trips and visits taking place, fieldwork had rarely been a strong feature of the curriculum before the pandemic. Leaders had not considered how fieldwork should be taught or how pupils would learn more about how geographers carry out their work.' Ofsted (2023)

To plan and undertake fieldwork effectively, geography leaders must consider where fieldwork features in the curriculum and how opportunities for fieldwork are sequenced over time.

When reflecting on the sequence of fieldwork within the curriculum, it is important to consider:

- Which year groups undertake fieldwork? Is there a balance across Key Stage 1 and Key Stage 2?
- How does the Early Learning Goal for People, Culture and Communities support pupils' understanding of the local area? How does this provide foundational knowledge and understanding for fieldwork in Key Stage 1?
- What fieldwork are pupils doing? Does the expectation of procedural knowledge/geographical skills increase as pupils learn and remember more?
- Where do pupils go for fieldwork and why?
- In which ways do pupils communicate their findings from fieldwork and is this sequenced across the curriculum?

When we consider the sequencing of fieldwork, we are ensuring that it happens (that we meet statutory requirements for the National Curriculum in England) and also that pupils can make progress over time. This avoids a situation where either no fieldwork is completed, or that fieldwork becomes 'a trip' with little geographical thinking embedded.

It is also helpful to consider when procedural knowledge is taught that pupils need to use whilst undertaking fieldwork. For example, if pupils already recognise and understand some commonly used symbols on OS maps, then they will be able to apply this knowledge and practise the skill of map reading when using an OS map to navigate during fieldwork.

In practice: example of <u>poorly</u> sequenced fieldwork within a primary curriculum

	Autumn A	Autumn B	Spring A	Spring B	Summer A	Summer B
KS1		Year 1 local area			Year 1 trip to Abbey Woods	
Lower KS2						Year 4 beach trip
Upper KS2				Year 5 local area		

'We have some geography trips, but I know we could have more. Year 1 walk to the post box to post their letters to Santa and that helps them to learn about the local area. They then do a trip to some woodland, which is really a science trip about habitats but there's a bit of geography too. Year 4 do a beach trip which links in with their English text. Year 5 do the local area again and plan a route to the local park.'

Reflections:

- Which specific features of the local area are Year 1 expected to recognise? Are they using locational and positional language, planning their route using a map, drawing any maps?

- Science and geography often overlap, how could the woodland trip maximise geography opportunities? Could pupils navigate within the woods using a compass? Do they use maps to locate places within the woods?

- When Year 4 do their beach trip, what are they learning about coastlines? Could they draw sketch maps of the area they visit? Are there any opportunities to gather data?

- Year 5 plan a route to the local park, is this challenging enough? Could they use four- and six-figure grid references to identify locations in the local area? Could they explore a particular relevant issue and gather data? How has their knowledge of the local area progressed from Year 1?

- Overall, how can we build in more opportunities for fieldwork, recognising budget constraints and maximising opportunities for fieldwork on the school site or in the local area?

In practice: example of more effectively sequenced fieldwork

	Autumn A	Autumn B	Spring A	Spring B	Summer A	Summer B
KS1	Year 1 local area (school site) Year 2 local area (Immediate local area beyond the school site)				Year 1 trip to Abbey Woods (compass, map drawing, symbols on maps)	Year 2 local area (planning and navigating a route to local park)
Lower KS2	Year 3 local area (focus on human and physical features and sketch maps) Year 4 local area (changes over time, historical maps, population change)		Year 3 rivers (local river, data collection on river depth)			Year 4 beach trip (including sketch maps of landscape and data collection on litter problem)

	Autumn A	Autumn B	Spring A	Spring B	Summer A	Summer B
Upper KS2				Year 5 local area (local study on specific issue – traffic data collection, graphing and presenting to local councillor)		Year 6 school journey (orienteering, compass, grid references, map work)

'Fieldwork features at least once in each year group and pupils learn and remember more as they work through the curriculum.

In Key Stage 1 the focus is on recognising and identifying features of the local area, using simple maps and becoming familiar with the local area. By the end of Key Stage 1 pupils use their knowledge of the local area to plan a route to a local park.

In lower Key Stage 2 pupils build on their knowledge from Key Stage 1 and look at physical and human features of the local area before learning about how our local area has changed over time. They use historical maps and compare them with what is located in our local area at present. When Year 3 study rivers, they undertake fieldwork where they measure the river depth at different points (we risk assess this as with any other fieldwork) then Year 4 undertake fieldwork on their beach trip where they draw maps and collect data to investigate the litter problem.

Year 5 learn more about the local area when they study a specific issue, this year it is traffic, but it might change if something locally relevant occurs next year. When Year 6 embark upon their residential, we've planned for them to do an orienteering task where they use a compass and a map to navigate to different locations in teams. This gives them a chance to apply their map skills they've learned in previous years. Our fieldwork has been planned to provide a strong foundation for future learning when our pupils move to secondary school.'

Reflections:

- Each year group has at least one opportunity for fieldwork, many of these are in the local area and therefore have very little/no cost implication.

- It is clear that fieldwork becomes more challenging over time as pupils learn and remember more and specific procedural knowledge/geographical skills are identified to guide teachers.
- The plan is realistic and achievable with tight budgets, and recognises that other subject areas will require trips and visits to enhance them.

What effective fieldwork looks like

'Through its unique nature fieldwork offers benefits to students that are of profound importance…It brings conceptual, cognitive, procedural and social gains, much of which would be lost without the particular opportunities fieldwork provides.'
(Lambert et al., 2014, p. 8)

Both the Royal Geographical Society and the Geographical Association are unequivocal in their support of fieldwork within the geography curriculum. In the 2009 manifesto: 'A different view', the Geographical Association stated, 'Fieldwork – that is, learning directly in the untidy real world outside the classroom – is an essential component of geography education.'

Often fieldwork can turn into a 'fun trip' which might have its own benefits but may lack in actual fieldwork. If we include engaging with maps, compasses, measurement tools and data collection, then we are on the right lines with planning effective geography fieldwork.

In practice: components of effective fieldwork

What are the components of effective fieldwork and how can we as leaders support staff to make this happen?

Component	Questions to ask	Examples
Defined purpose	During this fieldwork: What are pupils going to do? What will pupils be thinking about? What will pupils learn? Why have I chosen this location for fieldwork?	The purpose of the fieldwork is to explore our local river and find out where the flow is the fastest. Pupils will measure flow in the river at three points using a float and a stopwatch, working in groups of three. We have chosen this location because there are three points where the river is shallow enough for pupils to paddle in to measure the flow.

Component	Questions to ask	Examples
Procedural knowledge	Which geographical skills will pupils be using? When will they learn the procedural knowledge/ skills they need for the fieldwork?	Pupils will use their locational knowledge to identify where they need to take the three measurements using an OS map. Using measuring skills from maths, they will measure a two-metre section of river. They will use knowledge and skills from maths to use the stopwatch. Before the fieldwork, we will check pupils can use tape measures.
Information gathering	What information will pupils be looking for? Will pupils gather data? If so, is it quantitative (numerical) or qualitative (attitudes and opinions) data? Do pupils need to measure to gather data? Do pupils need to use any tools when measuring?	Pupils will be finding out where the river flows the fastest. They will gather numerical data based on the time it takes for a float to travel two metres. They will measure two metres at three different points of the river. They will use stopwatches to time the float.
Experiences	What will pupils have the opportunity to experience during the fieldwork?	Pupils will be standing in a shallow river. They will walk between three points in the river experiencing the journey of the river as it moves downstream. They will have time to explore the area.
Analysis and communication	What will pupils do with the products of their fieldwork? Will pupils draw diagrams or create graphs? When will these be taught? How will pupils communicate their findings from fieldwork?	Pupils will record their times in a table during the fieldwork. They will also draw sketch maps of the section of the river they work in. They could plot their results into a line graph, but a table may suffice for this task. They will create a report that describes and explains the path of the river using maps, sketch maps and the data they recorded.

Component	Questions to ask	Examples
Inclusion	What scaffolds and adaptations will be needed to ensure the experience of fieldwork is inclusive for all pupils?	A pupil with a physical disability will need support accessing the river. The risk assessment has identified the safest places for all pupils to enter the river, including where this individual can rest comfortably. Parents or carers will be consulted and the adult who works with the pupil will be briefed on additional safety measures, including maintaining appropriate physical contact whilst the pupil stands in the river. Key vocabulary that is relevant for this trip will be used in geography and maths lessons before we go. A language intervention group will use the key vocabulary as their focus the week before the fieldwork trip. A social story with photos (taken when undertaking the risk assessment) will be shared with a pupil who struggles with disruption to routine.

How to risk assess fieldwork

Schools are likely to have their own templates for risk assessing fieldwork, but it is essential that as a geography leader, you understand what is required by the risk assessment process so that you can support other members of staff and ensure the highest level of safety is maintained at all times during fieldwork.

The member of staff responsible for the fieldwork must conduct a risk assessment by visiting the area where the fieldwork takes place, planning an exact route and highlighting where risks may occur. Then steps must be taken to minimise risks, for example finding the safest place to cross a road, ensuring there are regular headcounts when joining or leaving public transport, finding the safest place to access a river.

The risk assessment for any geography fieldwork must be updated each time the trip will be undertaken to allow for any changes to the location or means of transport. The risk assessment should be signed off by a senior leader in line with school procedures.

In practice: example risk assessment

Below is an example risk assessment; teachers should use the templates provided by their own schools for their fieldwork and not consider this a comprehensive document to be used in schools.

Location:	Date:		Assessment completed by:	
What is the risk?	Who is at risk?	What is the risk level?	What can be done to reduce the risk?	Who is responsible for reducing the risk?
Example: Crossing oncoming traffic on Regent Street at the junction with Oxford Street	All	Medium	Cross at a pedestrian crossing. One adult in high-vis jacket to stand in the road whilst pupils cross on each side of the island. Pupils to line up in fours to cross the road promptly. One adult at the front and end of lines. Pupils briefed on road safety prior to the fieldwork.	All adults and pupils behaving appropriately, being mindful of road safety.

Location:	Date:		Assessment completed by:	
Example: Insect bites from long grass	All	Low	Pupils with allergies to insect bites identified and parents or carers briefed before the fieldwork. Pupils and adults told to wear long trousers for the fieldwork. Class teacher will carry a first aid kit and any medication for pupils with allergies.	All adults to watch for insect bites. Trained member of staff to administer medication for pupils with allergies.
Example: Drowning in river	All	Medium	All pupils and adults to be briefed on safety around the river before fieldwork and reminded directly before fieldwork. Pupils to enter the river only at designated locations (with shallow water) – teacher to indicate these with poles and flags. The depth of the river can change with rainfall – to be checked and measured by the class teacher before pupils enter.	All adults to supervise pupils at all times. Pupils responsible for safe behaviour.

Chapter summary

- In this chapter we have discussed the purpose of fieldwork, the role of procedural knowledge, sequencing fieldwork across the curriculum and components of effective fieldwork.

- Recognising the demands on time within primary schools and the many subjects taught, we must ensure there are opportunities for fieldwork within the curriculum.

- Maximising opportunities for fieldwork within your school site can help to provide learning experiences where pupils can apply their knowledge in an out of classroom context.

- Understanding the components of effective fieldwork will ensure you plan and undertake fieldwork with your pupils that helps them to understand the ways in which geographers work.

Questions for reflection

- Where do pupils do fieldwork in our school?
- Why have these places been chosen?
- What experiences do our pupils have when undertaking fieldwork?
- What procedural knowledge/skills will our pupils be using when they are conducting fieldwork?
- How do our pupils 'get better' at fieldwork as they move through the curriculum?

Example PD session: developing effective fieldwork

Here is an example of what a PD session on developing effective fieldwork could look like.

TIMING SUGGESTION	SESSION GUIDANCE
10 mins	Read the advice about fieldwork from the Royal Geographical Society.

TIMING SUGGESTION	SESSION GUIDANCE
5 mins	Discuss where fieldwork currently occurs within the curriculum and what pupils do when they are completing it.
15 mins	Use the components of effective fieldwork table from this chapter and ask teachers to consider one of their field trips through these lenses in different key stages. Identify how pupils progress with fieldwork. How does it get harder as they move through the curriculum?
20 mins	Give teachers the opportunity to plan their next fieldwork, using the components of effective fieldwork from this chapter.

Explore further

- The Geographical Association's *A different view: a manifesto from the Geographical Association* (2009)

- The Geographical Association's 'Fieldwork: Investigating habitats in our school grounds': https://geography.org.uk/resources/fieldwork-investigating-habitats-in-our-school-grounds/

- Royal Geographical Society's 'Fieldwork' in *Developing Primary Geography*: https://www.rgs.org/schools/resources-for-schools/guidance-and-support-in-developing-high-quality-primary-geography/fieldwork

- The Field Studies Council's *Teacher Resource Pack for Investigating Change in the School Grounds/Local Park* (2023): https://www.field-studies-council.org/wp-content/uploads/2023/06/KS3-Geography-The-School-Grounds-or-Local-Park.pdf

9 Assessment

Understanding what pupils know and understand and how much progress they are making has been a key part of teachers' roles throughout the history of education (Wyse et al., 2022). Assessment is a key part of any teacher's role, and as leaders of primary geography, we rely on assessment to give us a sense of how effective our subject is and what could be improved. Assessments should check what pupils know, check their understanding and ensure that pupils have remembered the curriculum content in the long term (Ofsted, 2021).

As primary teachers, we engage in both summative and formative assessments in a range of subjects. Summative assessments are assessments that review pupil attainment at a given point in time. In primary schools, there are statutory summative tests, for example the Multiplication Tables Check in Year 4 or the Mathematics National Curriculum Tests, commonly known as SATs tests in Year 6. We may also use non-statutory summative tests, perhaps that are part of a purchased scheme of work. Summative tests often give a score, providing numerical data that can be analysed.

In contrast to summative assessment, formative assessment is an ongoing, informal process that involves frequent assessments of learning that teachers make during lessons or in response to homework or other tasks. Formative assessment is an active process in which teachers check for understanding and are immediately responsive to the information they receive.

Both forms of assessment can offer insight into which pupils are learning successfully at the expected rate and which pupils have misconceptions or might need more support.

As primary geography leaders, we are interested in what both summative (if applicable) and formative assessments are telling us about pupils' achievement in geography. As leaders we might use other sources of information to assess the effectiveness of our subject, such as conducting pupil voice or capture information about teacher subject confidence from a staff survey. This higher-level assessment of our subject is how we find out what is working well and what we need to do to improve.

As you reflect on assessment methods in the classroom, it is important to keep in mind both the purpose of a particular assessment and the experience a pupil will have as the assessment is completed. Involving pupils in the assessment process is critical to their understanding of why they are completing a particular task, and clarity on the purpose and the components of an assessment will support them to succeed.

In this chapter, we will cover the following points as we explore assessment in geography:

- summative assessment (including the associated difficulties)
- formative assessment
- effective questioning
- designing effective assessment tasks.

Summative assessment

A summative judgement is one where we assign a child a score or a level, indicating in principle that they have reached a specific level of attainment. Primary geography does not have statutory summative assessments; there is no government-mandated test for geography. Some schools may have their own, internal summative assessment system for the foundation subjects. However, as Ofsted reported, 'In primary schools, teachers were often asked to make summative judgements about pupils' progress. However, these were not always underpinned by assessments that gave a sufficient or accurate picture of pupils' knowledge and skills' (Ofsted, 2023).

You may find yourself working within a system where teachers are expected to undertake summative assessments and, if this is the case it might be helpful to reflect on the following questions:

- What is the summative data needed for?
- How is the summative data used?
- What summative assessments are pupils undertaking?
- How accurate are the summative assessments?
- What is the workload implication of the summative assessments?

If we expect teachers to make summative judgements in geography, it is important to ensure that these are based on reliable and accurate assessments. This is an area fraught with challenges because a test in geography could be a rather blunt instrument, and it may not accurately capture what pupils know and can do. It is also very difficult to say if a pupil is working at an 'expected standard', without an ability to compare with a much larger group of pupils at the same stage.

When considering summative assessment, think about its accessibility for primary-aged pupils:

- What is the purpose of this summative assessment?
- If Year 1 pupils are expected to read assessment questions, can they do this independently?
- If the response to assessment questions is written, can pupils write well enough to answer the questions?
- Have pupils been taught all the content within an assessment so we are setting them up for success?
- Can any adaptations be made to the assessment to ensure pupils with SEND needs are well supported?
- What is a pupil's experience during this summative assessment?

Implications for teacher workload

In the school inspection handbook, Ofsted highlight, that when teachers use assessment effectively, it can help pupils to embed their knowledge and use it effectively. This can also help teachers to identify the next steps their pupil's need to take. However, Ofsted explain that, 'assessment is too often carried out in a way that creates unnecessary burdens for staff and pupils. It is therefore important that leaders and teachers understand its limitations and avoid misuse and overuse' (Ofsted, 2024).

When considering how teachers assess within geography, it is important to consider the workload implications of the assessments teachers are asked to complete. If thirty pupils sit a five-page geography assessment that teachers have to mark and then input data into a school system, this will require a lot of the teacher's time, just for one subject. It is, perhaps, worthwhile considering if this is a good use of time and if the same or similar information could be gathered another way.

Reporting data

It may be the case that you are asked to make summative judgements at a given point in the year and report some data for geography. It is important to recognise the difficulties with this approach. We can base judgements on work in pupil's books, but is it possible to do this accurately when tasks may have been heavily supported? Do tasks really reveal what pupils know and can do? We may take into account what we know about the children from class discussions, but again can we be accurate with these judgements? We need to be cautious when reporting data and consider how the data is generated.

Accuracy

Accuracy is an issue with summative assessments in primary schools for the reasons identified above. Assigning pupils a level or number in geography without any high-quality level descriptors is subjective and can lack accuracy. As a geography leader, it is important to understand the rationale for your assessment system within your subject. If you are required to undertake summative assessments, it is important to reflect on their accuracy and the value they bring to the school, parents or carers and pupils.

Formative assessment

Formative assessment is an ongoing process that frequently checks on pupils' understanding and makes adjustments as and when necessary in response to their learning. Unlike summative assessment, formative assessment is not data-led, but it *informs* us about pupils' knowledge and understanding.

Formative assessment relies on teachers clearly understanding what they want pupils to learn in geography. This helps to know where pupils are with their knowledge and understanding, where they are going and what steps they need to take to get there. It also helps identify misconceptions as and when they arise, allowing them to be addressed and resolved.

As geography leaders, we are responsible (with the support of senior leadership) for identifying the component knowledge within our curriculum. This will enable teachers to formatively assess pupils' progress regularly and frequently as they progress through the curriculum. It therefore needs to be clear what pupils should know and be able to do at each point in their curriculum journey.

Staff meeting time allocated to geography could be used to focus on formative assessment, how it is used and how it can be an effective tool for checking pupils' knowledge, understanding and progress in geography.

In practice: how to check for understanding using formative assessment

Here are some examples of how formative assessment can be used to check for understanding in geography.

Formative assessment tool	Implementation	Possible outcome	Reflection
Prior learning check	The teacher sets a prior learning check – asking pupils to answer questions on mini whiteboards about a previous unit on the UK. The teacher uses '3,2,1 show me' to check pupils' answers and get a sense of what they remember.	The teacher recognises that pupils' knowledge of the UK was strong but that many struggled to define the word 'coastline'. The teacher explains that coastline is where land meets the sea, shows some pictures and locates some key places in the UK near coastline on a map.	How do we check pupils' prior learning in our geography lessons? How are prior learning checks different across the key stages? Do pupils know why their prior learning is being checked?
Asking many questions	The teacher carefully plans questions to reveal misconceptions (for example questions about the difference between weather and climate) and asks pupils to answer them together on mini whiteboards to ensure maximum participation.	The teacher plans questions that will enable them to be responsive to any misconceptions and pupils are being asked to think deeply at many points throughout the lesson.	How do teachers use questioning in geography lessons? What do pupils understand about how they respond to questions?

Formative assessment tool	Implementation	Possible outcome	Reflection
Quizzing	The teacher implements a low stakes quiz in class using questions set up with plausible distractors to reveal any misconceptions. They also set an online quiz for homework with similar questions at the end of the week to find out what pupils remember.	The teacher realises that several pupils are making the same mistakes, so decides to reteach specific content to ensure everyone is secure. The teacher also recognises that a pupil who is new to English cannot read the quiz, so a version is produced with images to support understanding.	How can quizzes be used effectively in geography? Are quizzes formatted differently to support the needs of all learners? Do pupils know why they are completing quizzes?
Exit tickets	In upper KS2, a teacher poses a question that relates to the key learning objective for the lesson on slips of paper that pupils respond to before they leave at the end of the day. This is a quick check on pupils' understanding. The slips won't be kept (no need to add to workload). Example: 'Why is map projection challenging?'	The teacher checks the exit tickets to get a sense of what pupils understood to inform their next lesson and to identify which pupils may benefit from some extra input before moving on to new content.	How closely linked to the learning objective should an exit ticket be to make it most effective? Do pupils know how exit tickets support their learning?

Retrieval practice

'Most geography lessons include elements of retrieval practice, where pupils are expected to recall what they have learned. In schools where this is strongest, pupils

recall knowledge until they are fluent in it and then, later in the lesson, apply this knowledge in a new context. This helps them to make connections between lessons and between topics.' (Ofsted, 2023)

Any of the tools in the previous table can be used as retrieval practice in primary geography. This recall of previously taught content is essential to support learning and must become fluent if pupils are to draw upon it and use it in new contexts.

For example, pupils learn to identify the seven continents in Year 1. If pupils learn the continents effectively, they can identify them on a map of the world. For the rest of their primary geography education, when a new country and its continent are mentioned, pupils will have a mental map of the world in which they place this new knowledge.

Retrieval practice can also be a form of formative assessment as it tells us, as teachers, how secure pupils' understanding is at a given moment, which is useful information with which to shape our teaching.

Checking on procedural knowledge

In primary geography, formative assessments can focus on the substantive knowledge within the curriculum (for example place knowledge), but it must also check on pupils' procedural knowledge (sometimes referred to as geographical skills). This is the knowledge of how to 'do' something, for example how to calculate distance on a map, or how to use a grid reference to locate a point on a map.

Checking on procedural knowledge will help identify those pupils who need more support and those who are proficient and can apply their understanding in new contexts.

Effective questioning

Questioning is one of the key tools we use as teachers. If undertaken skilfully, questioning requires pupils to think deeply and gives insight into their understanding. Not only does questioning do these important things, but it also helps to develop our relationship with the pupils we teach as we show interest in their thoughts and opinions and value their contributions.

Kathleen Cotton's review of the research on questioning in the late 1980s explored the purposes of teacher questioning. Her insights remain useful today, and we can use her purposes of questioning to reflect on why and how we question in our primary geography lessons.

Purpose of questioning	Example questions
Interest, motivation and active involvement	Thinking about climate and weather, where might be a dangerous place to live in the world? What might it be like to live in a tropical climate? Have you ever visited a place that is different to where we live?
Evaluation of preparation work (for example homework)	What are some key geographical features of the place you researched for homework? (Using a visualiser to share a pupil's work): What can you tell us about your map?
Developing curiosity and critical thinking	Why are some plants and animals only found in certain parts of the world? How does flooding impact on people living in low-lying land? Why did farmers build rice terraces in the Philippines?
Reconnecting to previous learning	Last week we talked about weather. What are the differences between climate and weather? In the last unit we explored rivers. How does a river change as it journeys to the sea?
Exposing connections	What challenges might people face if they cannot find safe drinking water? How do hurricanes and tropical storms impact people who live in the Florida Keys? How does a country's natural resources effect it's economy?
Checking for progress against learning objectives	(Directly relating to a learning objective) Why is tourism important to the South west of England? Why is farming important in the south east of England? Can you name the seven continents?

Purpose of questioning	Example questions
Encouraging pupils to take their learning on further	What might a geographer notice about this new place? What other interesting places could we learn about? Can you find out what a geologist is interested in and why?

How to ask questions

Planning high-quality, purposeful questions is important, but we must also consider *how* we ask them to ensure maximum participation from the pupils in the classroom.

Ofsted found, 'Questioning in class often relied on pupils volunteering an answer. The understanding of the rest of the class was not checked' (Ofsted, 2023). This is a common scenario: a teacher asks a question, albeit a great question; pupils who think they know and answer and are confident to share put up their hands; those who don't know or are reluctant to share keep their hands down; one pupils is chosen and many are disappointed.

In practice: asking questions effectively

'Who can tell me what you might see in a port?'

'Yes, Yasmin.'

'You might see some boats with people taking cargo off and onto lorries.'
'Excellent answer.'

In this scenario, the teacher knows Yasmin understands what a port is, but the teacher cannot be sure what the rest of the class knows.

'We are going to talk to our partners and remember what we learned last lesson. Here is my question, 'what might you see in a port?' Turn and talk. (Pupils turn to talk to their partner.)

'Excellent, I heard lots of people mention boats and cargo ships. They both might be found in a port.

Now, using your whiteboards, I want you to write down what you might see in a port.'

All pupils are writing, a teaching assistant (TA) is supporting a pupil with speech and language delay by using picture prompts used in the previous lesson when discussing ports.

'Excellent, I am going to ask you to show me in 3, 2, 1…show me. Adil, you have remembered there could be cranes to move some of the cargo; well done for remembering the word ferries, Adam. Are ferries the same as cargo ships? No! My turn, your turn; ferries are boats that take passengers (class choral response).'

In this scenario, all pupils are working hard and thinking, and the teacher can judge who can confidently answer the question and who might need some more input. Pupils have had a chance to talk to their partner before they write on their whiteboards. This boosts confidence and helps those who may have forgotten. The teacher has checked on each pupil's understanding and can be responsive immediately.

Depth of questioning

It is useful to be aware of the depth of our questioning in geography. Sometimes we may ask simple, factual recall questions, for example 'what is the capital city of France?'. At other times, we might be asking questions that require deeper thinking, for example 'how are people in Malawi affected by food insecurity? Why was it necessary to build the Humber Bridge in this location?' Both types of questions are important, and both have their role in supporting pupils' understanding, but the important part of questioning is planning which questions to ask and when.

Rob Coe et al. identified questioning as one of the component parts of activating hard thinking in 'Great teaching toolkit evidence review', highlighting that questions and dialogue can be used to 'promote elaboration and connected, flexible thinking among learners' (Coe et al., 2020). They also emphasise the importance of 'getting responses from all students', therefore maximising participation, as we have mentioned.

In the following table you can see some important factual recall questions followed by probing questions that build on the initial factual recall to require harder thinking and to provide an opportunity for pupils to demonstrate the depth of their geographical understanding.

Factual recall	Deeper thinking
What is a climate zone?	How do climate zones affect agriculture around the world?
Where is the equator?	What would we expect the climate to be like in equatorial regions?
What is the capital city of England?	What factors influenced the location of London as a capital city?
Which countries are located in Europe?	How are countries in Europe similar and different?
What is the longest river in the UK?	How has the River Severn shaped land over time?
What is a desert?	What challenges might people who live at the edge of the Sahara Desert face?

Designing effective assessment tasks

The Ofsted subject report in 2023 identified that effective assessment in geography involves careful task design with 'both short responses, to check pupils' component knowledge, and longer tasks that allowed them to apply what they had learned to answer geographical questions' (Ofsted, 2023). This is a key principle for designing effective assessment tasks; creating a multifaceted approach to assessment recognising that one single task will not provide an accurate picture of what pupils know and can do.

Assessment tool	Example	Advantages	Considerations
Short questions	What is the capital city of Scotland?	Quick to administer, definitive answers (right or wrong), clearly identifies gaps in knowledge	Doesn't reveal depth of understanding
Longer questions	How is the landscape in Scotland diverse?	Requires deep thinking, offers an opportunity to apply knowledge, use subject specific vocabulary, apply geographical thinking, compare and contrast, write with disciplinary features	Takes time, requires teachers to scaffold and provide support for pupils who may struggle to write independently
Map tasks	Label this map of Scotland	Relatively quick to complete, reveals some locational knowledge	Pupils may just guess when labelling so may need to be encouraged to use an atlas if needed
Data tasks	Use this population map to describe population density in Scotland	Requires pupils to use and apply both mathematical and geographical skills, will identify if pupils can use a key effectively	Data sources need to be chosen carefully so there is no extra information that pupils won't understand – they need to be clear
Oral presentations	What would a geographer say about Scotland?	This requires pupils to show their geographical understanding without needing to write, pupils who find writing a challenge may be able to show what they know more effectively, pupils participate in communicating the geography they understand (an important part of the subject)	Pupils should plan their presentation and use the plans as scaffolds if needed It is important to build confidence and teachers should consider how pupils will present and to whom

When designing effective assessment tasks, we must know exactly what it is we are looking for and also know the components of the curriculum that pupils are learning to ensure we are setting them up for success. This will help us select assessment tasks that tell us what pupils know and can do, revealing specific gaps in learning and, therefore, helping us respond to any misconceptions or mistakes.

As geography leaders, we need to know how our subject is assessed and also how teachers use assessment information to inform their teaching. We also need to have a broad overview of what assessments tell us about our curriculum's strengths and weaknesses.

We might notice, for example, that pupils across the school are finding map tasks challenging. In response to this, we might check the atlas and map provision in school. Are teachers using these resources effectively? Are pupils engaging in map work frequently? Are the demands of map tasks increasing steadily as pupils learn and remember more?

As leaders, we must be aware of the themes we can draw from assessment and respond to these by adjusting and improving the curriculum.

Chapter summary

This chapter has explored:

- the challenges of summative assessment in primary geography and how you must question the accuracy of any summative data you use
- how formative assessment can help teachers to check for understanding as they teach primary geography
- how effective questioning can reveal gaps in knowledge and misconceptions that can then be addressed to help pupils make continued progress in primary geography
- the design of effective assessment tasks and how a multifaceted approach to assessment can provide a more accurate picture of pupils' knowledge and understanding.

Questions for reflection

- How do we assess in geography?
- What information do we gain from assessments?
- What do our pupils gain from completing the assessments?

- How do we use information gathered from assessments?
- How does assessment inform curriculum development within our school?

Example PD session: exploring assessment in geography

Here is an example of what a PD session on exploring assessment in geography could look like.

TIMING SUGGESTION	SESSION GUIDANCE
10 mins	Watch Dylan Wiliam's talk when he discusses formative assessment (Wiliam, 2020).
5 mins	Discussion: How do we use assessment in geography currently? When do we assess? What does it tell us? You may like to refer to the table in this chapter 'How to check for understanding using formative assessment'.
15 mins	In year groups or key stages, look at an example end of unit assessment lesson. Identify what kind of assessment is planned and what information that will tell us about what pupils know and can do. Look back at the unit of work and identify how each lesson contributes to the assessment task(s). Identify what pupils need to know to be successful in the assessment task(s).
20 mins	Give teachers time to reflect on their forthcoming assessment lessons across the year group they teach. What will we know about what pupils know and can do in geography by the end of the year? How will we know this?

Explore further

- Dylan Wiliam's talk 'What every teacher needs to know about assessment' (2020)
- Daisy Christodoulou's talk for Cambridge Assessment: 'Reclaiming formative assessment' (2012)
- *Assessing Progress in Geography* from The Geographical Association

10 Implementing change

Implementation is a key part of the role of a geography leader. Once we know what effective primary geography looks like, we must then make it happen in our schools. Implementation is the 'make it happen' part, which we know is not as straightforward as it sounds. We all want to improve the subjects we lead, but how do we do that in a way that brings everyone on board, with a shared focus that can be sustained long enough to have impact for the pupils we serve?

As a leader of geography, you will almost certainly be asked to write an action plan (sometimes called a development plan) each year to support the subject's strategic development. This helps you to focus on what you are seeking to change and how you will go about doing it.

It is important that your plan does the following:

- identifies the key priorities for geography
- lists specific actions to complete with timescales
- includes criteria, or ways of checking, that show the priority has been or is being successfully implemented.

It might be tempting to try to fix everything at once, but it is important to be realistic about your capacity and the resources available to effect change. Two or three priorities per year is a reasonable amount to focus on. Some priorities may take more than a year to implement and then see tangible change. This may mean you have a longer term plan, perhaps two or three years, underpinning your yearly plan. Your plan should be a working document, one you refer to during leadership time and one that provides a focus for your work as a leader of geography.

In this chapter we will explore:

- the challenges of implementation
- how to implement effective change.

The challenges of implementation

There is a strong chance, since you are reading this book, that you are already engaged in thinking deeply about primary geography and how to improve your subject offer. You might have some brilliant ideas and great vision for what you would like your pupils to be able to achieve. However, making a vision a reality is not straightforward and there can be many challenges to overcome before you can effect real change.

The Education Endowment Foundation identified that, 'Awareness of evidence does not necessarily result in improved outcomes' (Sharples et al., 2024, p.2). Knowing the evidence for improving something does not always translate into actual improvement. However, knowing the evidence is an essential part of any implementation journey, we want to know we are implementing changes with a sound evidence base. If we do not do this, we might be wasting time implementing something that will have little impact on pupil outcomes.

There are many challenges for a geography leader, some of these may include:

- **time** – as a foundation subject, geography may not be allocated much time in the school's professional development schedule and as a geography leader you may not be allocated a significant amount of leadership time

- **resources** – you may have a limited budget for resourcing your subject and for your own ongoing professional development; you may have inherited a curriculum that lacks structure or clarity

- **knowledge** – you may be leading a subject without expert geography knowledge yourself and it is highly likely you will be leading colleagues who do not have expert knowledge in geography; primary teachers cannot be experts in all of the twelve subjects they are responsible for teaching.

We must ensure our implementation of change in geography recognises these challenges and where possible removes barriers to effective change through careful planning. We know we won't suddenly have double the hours in the day, or a windfall financially, therefore we must work within the realities of our role.

How to implement effective change

The EEF make three clear recommendations which are helpful in the quest to implement effective change in primary geography:

- 'adopt the behaviours that drive effective implementation
- attend to the contextual factors that influence implementation
- use a structured but flexible implementation process.' (Sharples et al., 2024, p.5)

We are going to explore these in more detail, with examples of what this might look like in school. This will help you to shape your action/development plans and will cause you to reflect upon your leadership of geography and how you implement the change we want to see.

In practice: implementing effective change in primary geography

EEF's recommendation	Example in a primary geography context
'Adopt the behaviours that drive effective implementation'	1. Engage people by conducting a staff survey (this could be formal or just canvassing staff opinions by inviting them to send you their thoughts or meet for a conversation) to find out what staff think about geography and what their thoughts/concerns may be. 2. When you share a focus with staff, make it clear what the focus is, what changes will be made and explain the reasoning behind it. This will help to unite staff around a common goal. For example, we are going to focus on pupils' fieldwork as we identified in the survey that teachers feel they don't teach it frequently and have low confidence. Each teacher will identify where they teach fieldwork, and we will work together to build in specificity of geographical skills and to ensure progression across years in this area. We will check in on this each term to see how teachers and pupils are responding to this and make changes to implementation where needed. This focus will be identified in the subject action plan.

EEF's recommendation	Example in a primary geography context
'Attend to the contextual factors that influence implementation'	1. Staff will read the Geographical Association's fieldwork guidance, in order to be evidence informed, and in a staff meeting will discuss what fieldwork opportunities there are in the local area and which are practical for pupils of different ages. 2. Geography lead will share a template risk assessment for teachers to adapt to their specific fieldwork and will share a document outlining the progression of geographical skills across the curriculum so that teachers know what to focus on during fieldwork and how skills will build over time. 3. Geography lead will be released to attend fieldwork with an Early Career Teacher (ECT) to support.
'Use a structured but flexible implementation process'	1. Ensure the action/development plan identifies check-in points to ensure the work remains a priority throughout the year. This supports a structured by flexible implementation process. 2. Identify what practical steps must be taken to explore, prepare, deliver and sustain. Build in check-ins for 'sustain' into the two-/three-year plan to ensure change doesn't revert once attention moves on to new challenges. For example fieldwork may be at risk if busy teachers have other priorities. 3. Be willing to acknowledge where implementation has not had the expected impact, for example you may notice that children aren't using and applying subject specific vocabulary in the way you intended in lessons. So you may want to rethink how vocabulary is taught in geography.

Maintaining a dialogue with school leaders is important when setting and working on your plan for geography, as there may be aspects of your plan that fit in with wider school initiatives. For example, a school may be making an effort to move away from printed worksheets so you may decide to have an action point that relates to this in order for your work in geography to support implementation of an improvement across the school.

The EEF's four-phase approach for manageable implementation in schools

The EEF recommends a four-phase approach for manageable implementation in schools: 'explore, prepare, deliver and sustain' (Sharples et al., 2024, p.5). It is helpful for you as a geography leader to think about your action plan through these four lenses. You may want to consider:

- 'Explore' – *What do I know about geography in my school?* Your monitoring will allow you to identify strengths and areas for improvement in geography. You may gather evidence from book looks, lesson observations, pupil voice, staff and pupil surveys.
- 'Prepare' – *What is my plan for change?* You will need to consider how you will make an improvement; what practical steps are needed? You may need to identify success criteria.
- 'Deliver' – *How will I make this happen?* You will need to think about how you will support and encourage colleagues perhaps through training, dropping into planning meetings and modelling.
- 'Sustain' – *How will I ensure the change is embedded?* You will need to plan to review the change to ensure improvements are sustained over time.

In practice: considerations when preparing an action plan

The table below suggests some example areas of primary geography that could be helpful to consider when you are preparing an action plan.

Areas of primary geography	Targeted questions	Example action/ development plan priorities
National Curriculum coverage	Does our curriculum meet National Curriculum requirements? Is every class covering the content of their curriculum?	• Ensure all teachers are teaching the full curriculum. • Deliver support to any staff who are not teaching the full curriculum.

Areas of primary geography	Targeted questions	Example action/ development plan priorities
Sequencing and progression	How do pupils get better at geography? How does our curriculum support pupils to learn and remember more over time?	• Identify and articulate how pupils make progress within geography. • Share understanding of progression within geography with all teachers.
Vocabulary	How is vocabulary taught in geography? Can pupils apply newly learned vocabulary in their independent tasks and in conversations?	• Observe and evaluate the teaching of subject-specific vocabulary in geography. • Explore how well pupils use and apply newly learned vocabulary.
Map work	When is map work taught across the curriculum? How do pupils get better at map work as they progress through the curriculum?	• Identify where map work features in the school curriculum. • Ensure map work becomes more challenging as pupils move through the curriculum.
Fieldwork	Where does fieldwork feature in our geography curriculum? What knowledge and skills do pupils gain when they participate in fieldwork at each key stage?	• Identify where fieldwork features within the curriculum. • Identify the geographical skills pupils develop within fieldwork and ensure progression is built into the curriculum.
Resourcing	Do we use atlases in school? Are atlases accessible to teachers to use in lessons? Do all pupils access atlases in lessons? Do we use OS maps in school? Do all classes have maps of the UK, maps of the world and globes for pupils to refer to? Do we have access to any digital mapping tools?	• Audit geography resources. • Survey staff/pupils to find out how confident they are using geography resources, such as OS maps. • Ensure all classes have access to the resources required to deliver the full curriculum.

The case study that follows focuses on how the geography lead of a primary school in London improved writing in geography.

Case study: West London and Earl's Court Free School Primaries

Humanities Lead: Robert Kron

I lead geography at a school that has developed its own curriculum. We are constantly in the process of revising our practice. I support staff to get to grips with the substantive knowledge they teach and in doing so I try to catch any discrepancies between planning and implementation. I also keep an eye out for any key misconceptions that crop up in the pupils' work.

Explore

I have spent the majority of my career in upper Key Stage 2 and have always found monitoring invaluable for getting a broader, whole-school picture of progress from EYFS to Year 6. The basic tools of monitoring have been the most effective for improving geography: frequent low-stakes book looks, pupil voice, and observations, along with constant reflection.

Recently, using planning checks and book looks, I realised that despite teaching extremely ambitious content, the tasks pupils were completing in geography did not allow them to apply their knowledge in a way that was true to the discipline. Many of the writing tasks in geography involved things like creating tour brochures, writing diary entries or pretend weather reports; all of these tasks were in an effort to make the learning 'fun', but were, perhaps, doing geography itself a disservice.

Prepare

Since then, we have stripped back and redesigned most of the writing outcomes in geography. Perhaps the single biggest change in our attitude to the tasks set has been to carefully consider what we actually want them to demonstrate – not hope that a fun task accidently demonstrates high-level learning. We have carefully considered what makes good writing in geography and we planned staff meetings where I could deliver the key knowledge teachers needed. I worked with the English lead to align the expectations for writing in geography with the expectations for writing in English.

Deliver

We are now deliberate and explicit in teaching the disciplinary aspects of geography. We directly teach what makes geography unique as a subject and why its knowledge might be different from that found in history or literature. Vitally, we explicitly teach how to _write like a geographer_. The pupils themselves are, of course, not subject experts, nor do we expect them to be. We do however plan for each task to meet certain requirements:

- to be written with a formal tone
- to be written in the third person
- to contain the vocabulary specific to the topic itself
- to weave maps, data and statistics (where relevant) naturally into the writing.

I delivered initial training on this and when I have release time for geography, I drop into planning meetings and touch base with staff to ensure they are confident. Getting people on board with this change was key. I wanted them to see that writing across the curriculum can be valued and that literacy is more than just something pupils do in English!

Sustain

When we come to the end of a unit, we often set aside a week of English lessons to be used in structuring a longer report or essay with the proper tone and language. We have seen the outstanding level of work that all pupils, regardless of background, can produce and we have faith in the fact that the geography knowledge itself is rich and engaging. This work is not finished. We will keep monitoring the quality of writing in geography and sustain this positive change whilst we focus on other areas for improvement.

Chapter summary

In this chapter we have looked at the components of a successful implementation approach in primary geography. We have explored how leaders must:

- consider how to effectively implement the geography curriculum and any improvements intended
- think deeply about the school context when planning for implementation of improvements
- ensure that implementation is regularly checked on and that flexibility is built in to changes to allow leaders to respond to the needs of the school.

Questions for reflection

- What is the process for implementing change within a subject in our school?
- How could this process incorporate guidance from the EEF on effective implementation?
- How do we explore, prepare, deliver and sustain change in primary geography?

Explore further

- The EEF's *A School's Guide to Implementation* (2024) by J. Sharples, J. Eaton and J. Boughelaf
- The EEF's 'Examples of implementation plans' from Putting Evidence to Work: *A School's Guide to Implementation*: https://d2tic4wvo1iusb.cloudfr ont.net/production/eef-guidance-reports/implementation/EEF-Exam ple-of-Implementation-Plans.pdf
- The EEF's: 'Implementation theme – active ingredients' from *Putting Evidence to Work: A School's Guide to Implementation*: https://d2tic4wvo1i usb.cloudfront.net/eef-guidance-reports/implementation/EEF-Active-Ingr edients-Summary.pdf?v=1635355218

- Evidence for Learning's *Insights into de-implementation* resources: https://evidenceforlearning.org.au/support-for-implementation/school-planning-and-recovery/de-implementation
- The Best Practice Network's explanation of implementation: https://www.bestpracticenet.co.uk/news/the-implementation-process#:~:text=The%20four%20crucial%20steps%20of,about%20meaningful%20change%20and%20improvements
- *Thinking critically about educational claims* resources from That's a Claim!: https://thatsaclaim.org/educational/
- The University of Washington Department of Global Health's *What is implementation science?*: https://impsciuw.org/implementation-science/learn/implementation-science-overview/#:~:text=Implementation%20science%20is%20the%20scientific,use%20by%20practitioners%20and%20policymakers

Bibliography

Adichie, C. N. (2009), 'The danger of a single story'. *TED talk*, https://www.ted.com/talks/chimamanda_ngozi_adichie_the_danger_of_a_single_story.

Association Montessori Internationale (nd), 'Biography of Maria Montessori'. *montessori-ami.org*, https://montessori-ami.org/resource-library/facts/biography-maria-montessori.

Ausubel, D. P. (1968), *Educational Psychology: A Cognitive View*. New York: Holt. Rinehart and Winston Inc.

Baddeley, A. D. and Hitch, G. (1974), 'Working memory' in Bower, G. H. (ed), *The Psychology of Learning and Motivation: Advances in Research and Theory* (Vol. 8). New York: Academic Press, pp. 47-89.

Baddeley, A.D. (2003), 'Working memory: looking back and looking forward'. *Nature Reviews Neuroscience*, 4, 829–839.

Bjork, R. A and Bjork, E.L, (1992), 'A new theory of disuse and an old theory of stimulus fluctuation' in Healy, A., Kosslyn, S. and Shiffrin. R. (eds) (1992), *Essays in honor of William K. Estes, Vol. 1. From learning theory to connectionist theory; Vol. 2. From learning processes to cognitive processes*. Mahwah, NJ: Lawrence Erlbaum Associates, Inc, pp.35-67.

Boardman, D. (1989), 'The development of graphicacy: children's understanding of maps'. *Geography*, 74 (4), 321–331.

Burnett, L., Brack, S. and Anderson, S. (2021), 'Teaching about a place? Stop and think first!' *Decolonising Geography*, https://decolonisegeography.com/blog/2021/04/teaching-about-a-place-stop-and-think-first/.

Casey, E. S. (1997), *The Fate of Place: A Philosophical History*. University of California Press: Berkley, CA.

Catling, S. (1979), 'Maps and cognitive maps: the young child's perception'. *Geography*, 64 (4) 288–293.

Catling, S. (2013), 'The need to develop research into primary children's and schools' geography'. *International Research in Geographical and Environmental Education*, 22 (3), 177–182.

Christodoulou, D. (2012), 'Reclaiming formative assessment'. *Cambridge University Press & Assessment YouTube channel*, https://www.youtube.com/watch?v=aJco-frAql8.

Coe, R., Rauch, C. J., Kime, S. and Singleton, D. (2020), *Great teaching toolkit evidence review*. Sunderland: Evidence Based Education.

Cook, V. A. (2011), 'The origins and development of geography fieldwork in British schools'. *Geography*, 96 (2), 69–74.

Cotton, K. (1988), 'Classroom questioning'. *Education Northwest*, https://educationnorthwest.org/sites/default/files/ClassroomQuestioning.pdf.

Cowan, N. (2001), 'The magical number 4 in short-term memory: a reconsideration of mental storage capacity'. *Behavioral and Brain Sciences*, 24 (1), 87–185

Cresswell, T. (2008), 'Place: encountering geography as philosophy'. *Geography*, 93 (3), 132–139.

Cresswell, T. (ed) (2014), *Place: an introduction*. Chichester: Wiley-Blackwell.

Cuthbert, A. S. and Standish, A. (eds) (2021), *What Should Schools Teach? Disciplines, Subjects and the Pursuit of Truth*. London: UCL Press.

De Bruyckere, P., Kirschner, P. A. and Hulshof, C. D. (2015), *Urban Myths about Learning and Education*. London: Academic Press.

Department for Education (DfE) (2013), *National Curriculum in England: Key Stages 1 and 2 Framework Document*. London: Department for Education.

Department for Education (DfE) (2014), *Early Years Foundation Statutory Framework*. London: Department for Education.

Department for Education (DfE) and Department of Health (DoH) (2014), *Special Educational Needs and Disability Code Of Practice: 0 to 25 years*. London: Department for Education and Department of Health.

Dunn, K. and Darlington, E. (2016), 'Making resources accessible to visually impaired students'. *Teaching Geography*, 41 (1), 34–36.

Eaton, J. (2022), 'Moving from 'differentiation' to 'adaptive teaching'. *EEF blog*, https://educationendowmentfoundation.org.uk/news/moving-from-differentiation-to-adaptive-teaching.

Ebbinghaus, H. (1885), *Memory: a contribution to experimental psychology*. New York, NY: Dover.

Education Endowment Foundation (EEF) (2021), *Teaching and Learning Toolkit: an accessible summary of education evidence*. London: Education Endowment Foundation.

Education Endowment Foundation (EEF) (2024), *Using Research Evidence: A Concise Guide*. London: Education Endowment Foundation.

Education Endowment Foundation (EEF) (2024a), *Communication and language: approaches and practices to support communication and language development in the early years*. London: Education Endowment Foundation.

Enser, M. (2020), 'Interweaving Geography'. *Teaching Geography*, 45(1), 15-17.

Epstein, A. S. (2009), *Me, You, Us: Social-Emotional Learning in Preschool*. Ypsilanti, MI: HighScope Press.

Esri (2021), 'Enrich your teaching with GIS: free, game changing tools for teachers and students'. *Teach with GIS*, https://teachwithgis.co.uk/.

Field Studies Council (nd), *Investigating Change in the School Grounds/Local Park* Teacher Resource Pack. Shrewsbury: Field Studies Council. https://www.field-studies-council.org/wp-content/uploads/2023/06/KS3-Geography-The-School-Grounds-or-Local-Park.pdf

Gathercole, S. E. and Alloway, T. P. (2007), *Understanding working memory: a classroom guide*. London: Harcourt Assessment.

Geographical Association (nd), 'Place in geography'. *Geographical Association website*, https://geography.org.uk/ite/initial-teacher-education/geography-support-for-trainees-and-ects/learning-to-teach-secondary-geography/geography-subject-teaching-and-curriculum/geography-knowledge-concepts-and-skills/place-and-places/place-in-geography/.

Geographical Association (nd), 'Teaching place knowledge'. *Geographical Association website*, https://geography.org.uk/ite/initial-teacher-education/geography-support-for-trainees-and-ects/learning-to-teach-secondary-geography/geography-subject-teaching-and-curriculum/geography-knowledge-concepts-and-skills/place-and-places/teaching-place-knowledge/.

Geographical Association (nd), 'Planning a high quality geography curriculum'. *Geographical Association website*, https://geography.org.uk/planning-a-high-quality-primary-geography-curriculum/.

Geographical Association (nd), 'Assessing progress in geography'. *Geographical Association website*, https://geography.org.uk/curriculum-support/progression-and-assessment-in-geography/assessing-progress/.

Geographical Association (nd), 'Fieldwork: Investigating habitats in our school grounds'. *Geographical Association website*, https://geography.org.uk/resources/fieldwork-investigating-habitats-in-our-school-grounds/.

Geographical Association (2009), *A different view: a manifesto from the Geographical Association*. Sheffield: Geographical Association.

Goldacre, B. (2013), *Building Evidence into Education*. London: Department for Education.

Grenier, J. (2020), *Working with the Revised Early Years Foundation Stage: Principles into Practice*. London: Sheringham Nursery School and Children's Centre.

Haslam, J. and Shaw, A. (2019), *Engaging with evidence guide*. York: Institute for Effective Education.

Hattie, J. and Yates, G. (2013), *Visible Learning and the Science of How We Learn*. London: Routledge.

Hattie, J. (2017), 'Dispelling educational myths'. Science of Learning Research Centre.

Higgins, S., Martell, T., Waugh, D., Henderson, P. and Sharples, J. (2021), *Improving literacy in Key Stage 2: Guidance report*. London: Education Endowment Foundation.

Jackson, P. (2006), 'Thinking geographically'. *Geography* 91 (3), 199–204.

Jones, M. (ed) (2017), *The Handbook of Secondary Geography*. Sheffield: Geographical Association.

Jones, M. and Lambert, D. (eds) (2018), *Debates in Geography Education* (2nd edition). Abingdon: Routledge.

Kirschner, P. A. and Hendrick, C. (2020), *How Learning Happens: Seminal Works in Educational Psychology and What They Mean in Practice*. Abingdon: Routledge.

Lambert, D. (2011), 'Reviewing the case for geography and the 'knowledge turn' in the English national curriculum'. *The Curriculum Journal*, 22, 3.

Lambert, D. and Reiss, M. J. (2014), *The place of fieldwork in geography and science qualifications*. London: Institute of Education.

Macular Society (2025), 'General tips for teaching vision impaired students'. *Macular Society website*, https://www.macularsociety.org/professionals/teaching-resour ces/general-tips.

Madan, C. R. and Singhal, A. (2012), 'Using actions to enhance memory: effects of enactment, gestures, and exercise on human memory'. *Front Psychology*, 19 (3), 507.

Major and Higgins (2019), *What Works?* London: Bloomsbury Education.

Mee, K. J. and Wright, S. (2009), 'Geographies of belonging: Why belonging? Why geography?' *Environment and Planning A*, 41(4), 772–779.

Montessori Academy (2017), 'Material spotlight: the Montessori sandpaper globe'. *Montessori Education, Program & Practice*, https://montessoriacademy.com.au/ montessori-sandpaper-globe.

NASEN (nd), 'Differentiation – why and how?' *NASEN*, https://www.egfl.org.uk/sites/ default/files/Services_for_children/SEND/Differentiation%20Nasen.pdf

National Deaf Children's Society (2020), 'Deaf-friendly teaching: for primary school staff'. *National Deaf Children's Society*, https://www.ndcs.org.uk/documents-and-resources/deaf-friendly-teaching-for-primary-school-staff/.

National Geographic Society (2025), 'Here be dragons'. *National Geographic*, https://education.nationalgeographic.org/resource/here-be-dragons/

Nuthall, G. (2007), *The Hidden Lives of Learners*. Wellington: New Zealand Council for Educational Research (NZCER) Press.

Ofsted (2011), 'Geography: learning to make a world of difference'. *Ofsted*, https:// www.gov.uk/government/publications/geography-learning-to-make-a-world-of-difference.

Ofsted (2021), 'Research review series: geography'. *Ofsted*, https://www.gov.uk/gov ernment/publications/research-review-series-geography/research-review-ser ies-geography#forms-of-geographical-knowledge.

Ofsted (2023), 'Getting our bearings: geography subject report'. *Ofsted*, https://www. gov.uk/government/publications/subject-report-series-geography/getting-our-bearings-geography-subject-report.

Ofsted (2024), 'School inspection handbook'. *Ofsted*, https://www.gov.uk/governm ent/publications/school-inspection-handbook-eif/school-inspection-handb ook-for-september-2023.

Ordnance Survey (n.d.), 'Mapzone'. *Ordnance Survey*, https://www.ordnancesurvey. co.uk/mapzone/map-skills.

Ordnance Survey (2023), 'OS history: discover the history of Ordnance Survey'. *Ordnance Survey*, https://www.ordnancesurvey.co.uk/about/history.

Owens, P. (2021), 'Teaching map skills to inspire a sense of place and adventure'. *Ordnance Survey*, https://www.ordnancesurvey.co.uk/documents/resources/teach ing-map-skills-primary.pdf.

Owens, P. (2023), 'Maps and mapping in the early years: teaching map skills to inspire a sense of place and adventure in the early years'. *Ordnance Survey*, https://www.ordnancesurvey.co.uk/documents/resources/maps-and-mapp ing-in-the-early-years.pdf.

Perry, T., Lea, R., Jørgensen, C.R., Cordingley, P., Shapiro, K. and Youdell, D. (2021), *Cognitive Science Approaches in the Classroom: a review of the evidence*. London: Education Endowment Foundation.

Robertson, M., Maude, A. and Kriewaldt, J. (2019), 'Aligning mapping skills with digitally connected childhoods to advance the development of spatial cognition and ways of thinking in primary school geography'. *Geographical Education*, 32, 15–25.

Royal Geographical Society (nd), 'Starting to plan primary geography'. *RGS*, https://www.rgs.org/schools/resources-for-schools/guidance-and-support-in-develop ing-high-quality-primary-geography/starting-to-plan-primary-geography.

Royal Geographical Society (nd), 'Map skills'. *RGS*, https://www.rgs.org/schools/ resources-for-schools/map-skills.

Royal Geographical Society (nd), 'Fieldwork'. *RGS*, https://www.rgs.org/schools/ resources-for-schools/guidance-and-support-in-developing-high-quality-primary- geography/fieldwork.

Sayer, C. M. and Doherty, M.J. (2023), 'Understanding of spatial correspondence does not contribute to representational understanding: evidence from the model Room and false belief tasks'. *Dev Psychol*, 59(5):976-986.

Scoffham, S. and Owens, P. (2017), *Teaching Primary Geography*. London: Bloomsbury.

Sharples, J., Eaton, J. and Boughelaf, J. (2024), *A School's Guide to Implementation: Guidance Report*. London: Education Endowment Foundation.

Shibli, D. and West, R. (2018), 'Cognitive load theory and its application in the classroom'. *Impact*, https://my.chartered.college/impact_article/cognitive-load- theory-and-its-application-in-the-classroom/.

Sweller, J. (1988), 'Cognitive load during problem solving: effects on learning'. *Cognitive Science*, 12, 257–285.

Training and Development Agency for Schools (TDA) (2009), *Including pupils with SEN and/or disabilities in primary geography*. Manchester: Training and Development Agency for Schools.

The Schoyen Collection, 'Cylcon (yurda), possibly with map of Darling River'. *The Schoyen Collection*, https://www.schoyencollection.com/24-smaller-collections/maps/cylcon-darling-river-ms-5087-36.

Weinstein, Y. and Sumeracki, M. (2019), *Understanding How we Learn*. Abingdon: Routledge.

Wiliam, D. (2012), 'Every teacher can improve'. *Northwest Evaluation Association*, https://www.youtube.com/watch?v=eqRcpA5rYTE.

Wiliam, D. (2020), 'What every teacher needs to know about assessment'. *Dylan Wiliam*, https://www.youtube.com/watch?v=waRX-lOR5vE.

Wyse, P.D., Bradbury, P.A. and Trollope, R. (2022), 'Assessment for Children's Learning: A new future for primary education'. *ICAPE*, https://www.icape.org.uk/reports-and-research/reports/2/view.

Index